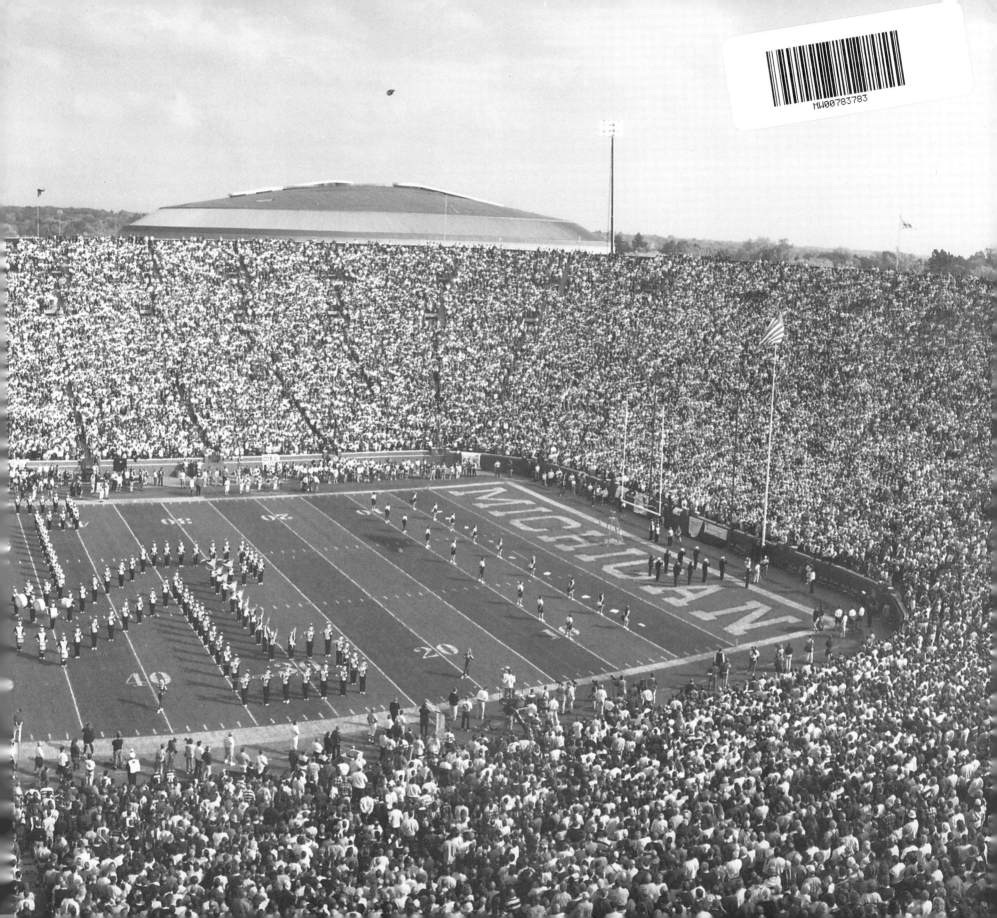

MICHIGAN FOOTBALL
YESTERDAY & TODAY ™

GEORGE CANTOR
FOREWORD BY JIM BRANDSTATTER

WEST
SIDE
PUBLISHING

George Cantor, a longtime Detroit newspaper columnist, saw his first game at Michigan Stadium in 1955. Since then, he has been caught up in the historic sweep of Michigan football, writing several books on the subject.

Jim Brandstatter has been a Michigan sportscaster since his graduation from the University of Michigan in 1972. As an offensive lineman under coach Bo Schembechler, he helped the Wolverines win two Big Ten titles and competed in two Rose Bowls.

Factual verification by Mitchell Light.

Special thanks to the following: archivist Greg Kinney of the Bentley Historical Library, for providing historical images of Michigan football; Michelle O'Brien, for her image research at Bentley; *The Michigan Daily*, for granting permission to reproduce its pages; Brian Snider, for allowing images of his Michigan football collection to be photographed; and Jean Hoyle, for photographing Michigan football memorabilia.

The Michigan marching band was the first-ever winner of the Sudler Trophy, awarded annually to the greatest band in the land.

Contents

U-M football fan   p. 21

Tom Harmon   p. 32

1969 OSU-Michigan game   p. 64

Coach Bo Schembechler p. 63

Brian Griese p. 113

Braylon Edwards p. 132

Foreword

I have been very fortunate, call it lucky, to have spent a great deal of my time at Michigan Stadium in Ann Arbor. In 1968 I enrolled at the University of Michigan and was on a freshman team that practiced in the great stadium. Back in those days, freshmen weren't allowed to play on the varsity squad, but just practicing in the great empty arena was a thrill.

In 1969 I got my first chance to play in a game. To run under the "M GO BLUE" banner in my winged helmet to the roar of 100,000 fans was a dream come true. After three years, 29 victories, two Big Ten titles, and two Rose Bowls, I graduated and moved on with life.

That new life, though, involved sports broadcasting. I loved the game of football, and of course I loved Michigan football. To stay involved with the program after I was finished as a player was an opportunity too good to be true. So, my career choice as a host

Jim Brandstatter

of the Michigan football coach's show, and a radio analyst on Wolverine games, was a no-brainer. I have never, ever regretted that choice.

One of my all-time favorite memories was the 1969 Ohio State-Michigan game. The Buckeyes were the scourge of the country. They were coming off a national championship in 1968, and they hadn't been beaten in 1969. When they came to play us, they were more than a two-touchdown favorite. They were ranked No. 1 in the nation. The conventional thinking was that Ohio State could compete with some NFL teams at the time.

But, we knew as a team that we could win. We believed it. When we beat them 24–12 in one of the greatest upsets in Michigan history, tears were shed and vindication was ours. Coach Bo Schembechler had told us that week, "What the mind can conceive, the body can achieve." Nothing can compare to that feeling of accomplishment and triumph. We knew as a team that we had made history. We had made those who had preceded us proud. We had set a higher standard for those who followed. We had woven our own thread into the fabric of the Michigan tradition.

As a broadcaster, the memories of great Michigan players and games seem to overlap. But there are moments I will never forget, such as the 1984 Sugar Bowl against Auburn. They had a backfield of Bo Jackson, Lionel James, and Tommie Agee, all of them destined for NFL stardom, and yet Michigan didn't allow a touchdown in that game. Michigan was outmanned and outsized, but with effort, heart, and pure tenacity, the Wolverines didn't allow Auburn's great offense to cross the goal line. Even though Michigan lost the game 9–7, it was the greatest single defensive effort I've ever seen.

I'll never forget 1979 when a freshman named Anthony Carter went into the huddle on the final play of a tie game against Indiana and told quarterback John Wangler, "Throw me the ball!" So Wangler did, and Anthony made a play that will live forever in Michigan history. Carter made the catch, split two defenders, avoided a shoestring tackle, and danced into the end zone as time expired to rescue a Michigan victory. It doesn't get any better than that!

How about Charles Woodson, during the 1997 national championship season, rising above five Michigan State players to make a one-handed interception that put the game away? How about Desmond Howard leaving his feet and launching himself parallel to the ground to make an impossible touchdown catch against Notre Dame that won the game in 1991? Or how about Lloyd Carr standing in the Rose Bowl locker room on January 1, 1998, after a 21–16 win over Washington State, saying to his exhausted team with emotion choking his voice, "Men, you have left a lasting legacy. You have just won the national championship!"

> Scriptwriters can't come up with these stories. They are written by young men who wear the maize and blue. In the heat of competition, they accomplish the extraordinary.

I was there and witnessed these incredible moments. I had the responsibility to relate these events to our listeners as a broadcaster. I can't remember what I said, and I'm sure I didn't do them justice. Who could? These things don't happen in movies. Scriptwriters can't come up with these stories. They are written by young men who wear the maize and blue. In the heat of competition, they accomplish the extraordinary.

Michigan football has been a great part of my life for 40 years now, and over those years I have grown to appreciate the history and tradition of the program even more. The opportunity for you to enjoy this rich story is now yours in the following pages of this book.

The most important part of tradition is history. The Wolverine program has a history that goes all the way back to the late 1800s. Coach Fielding H. Yost built a dynasty in the early 1900s, and his impact is still felt in the 21st century thanks to his foresight in building Michigan Stadium. Yost set the foundation of a football program that has recorded more wins, and been watched by more people, than any other collegiate football program in history.

It is difficult to capture feelings and emotion on paper. George Cantor is a writer who has the talent to accomplish this difficult job. He will escort you into the great stadium, where you will take your seat and relive the exploits of Willie Heston, Bennie Oosterbaan, Tom Harmon, Bump Elliott, Anthony Carter, and countless others as your maize and blue blood rises with pride and appreciation.

The great Michigan football broadcaster Bob Ufer used to say, "Football is a religion, and Saturday at Michigan Stadium is a holy day of obligation." Bob couldn't have been more accurate. Cantor has captured that feeling in this exciting book. In the pages that follow, you'll learn why Michigan football is the leader and best.

Enjoy!

Jim Brandstatter

Jim Brandstatter

Jim Brandstatter played offensive tackle under Bo Schembechler from 1969 to '71. He is the color commentator on Michigan football radio broadcasts, and he has cohosted Michigan Replay *since 1980.*

Champions of the West

1879–1926

Fielding H. Yost transforms football at Michigan from a leisurely pastime to a national sensation with a succession of championship teams. The stars, the music, the marching band, and the winning tradition are all set in place as Michigan builds the foundation that fans of the Wolverines cherish today.

Above: *Coach Fielding "Hurry Up" Yost ran practices at a breakneck pace, as evidenced by this 1904 image. Michigan outscored its opponents 567–22 that season, which included a 130–0 pasting of West Virginia.* Opposite page: *Medical student William McCauley* (standing, third from right) *coached Michigan to an 8–1 record in 1895, losing only to Harvard, 4–0.*

Birth of a Tradition

In the spring of 1879, a group of 12 young men from the University of Michigan boarded a train to Chicago. They were on their way to meet a similar party from Racine College for the purpose of playing a game of football. Michigan won 1–0.

It was not a game that anyone seated in Michigan Stadium today would recognize. Its organizers still hadn't decided whether it was supposed to resemble rugby or soccer. One player was, in fact, designated as the goalkeeper, and they lined up eight rushers and two halfbacks. The ball was round, no line of scrimmage existed, and kicking was the accepted way of advancing down the field.

But it was a beginning. It was the first football game in Michigan history, and—by some accounts—the first between two universities west of the Alleghenies.

They may have been neophytes, but the gridders were eager to learn. Within two years, the team arranged a trip east. There they played the powerhouses of Harvard, Yale, and Princeton, all within five days. Michigan lost all three games, but the players saw how this new game was played at its highest level.

Michigan did not have a coach, and it was the captain's job to arrange contests. Some seasons included as few as one or two games, which made it fairly easy for Michigan to go unbeaten for four consecutive years in the 1880s.

Michigan students had referred to themselves as Wolverines since the 1860s, and the name gradually became

attached to the team. Very few, if any, of those fierce little animals had ever roamed the woodsy state. However, Michigan was known as the Wolverine State, and the university felt that it was a fine team nickname, too. The colors of maize and blue had been associated with the school since 1867, when a student committee recommended they be adopted as "emblematic."

By 1891 Michigan was playing a schedule of nine games, and five years later it became a charter member of the Western Conference. The national press wasn't paying much attention. All that mattered were the games

This 1884 team kicked off a mini dynasty for the Wolverines. They won all ten of their games from 1884 to 1887 while outscoring their opponents 258–10.

On the strength of his dominant performance against the University of Chicago in 1898, center William Cunningham was named an All-American, becoming the first Michigan player to be so honored.

between Harvard, Yale, Princeton, and Penn. Everything else was minor league.

That began to change in 1898, when Michigan played the biggest game in its brief history. The Wolverines were 9–0, and the finale was against its greatest rival. The scenario sounds familiar, but back then the team Michigan had to beat was the University of Chicago.

That school was a parvenu, in existence for less than a decade. It had the gall to hire a full-time salaried coach, Amos Alonzo Stagg. Unheard of! Worse yet, the Maroons had ruined unbeaten seasons for Michigan the previous two years. Excitement was intense as the big game approached, and two special trains were reserved to carry students and fans to Chicago.

On a frigid November day, Michigan trailed Chicago 11–6 in the fourth quarter. Then halfback Charles Widman burst free from a pile of players and raced 65 yards for the tying touchdown (worth five points back then). With the extra point, the Wolverines clinched a 12–11 victory and were the undefeated champions of the West.

That phrase sounded good to music student Louis Elbel, who was in the frenzied crowd. "We were crazed with joy," he said later. "My spirits were so uplifted that I was clear off the Earth, and that is when 'The Victors' was inspired."

Elbel completed work on the new song on the ride back to Ann Arbor, and the next Monday *The Michigan Daily* published the lyrics on page one. Result: An instant classic. One of the great pieces of Michigan tradition was now in place.

The Band Plays "The Victors"

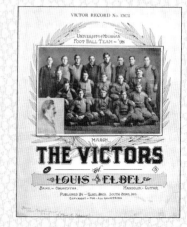

What good is a great song like "The Victors" unless there is a band to play it? Fortunately, that problem had been addressed. The first version of the Michigan marching band, 35 men strong (women weren't allowed in until 1972), was introduced to fans during the 1897 season. It even accompanied the team to Detroit for a game.

After the big win at Chicago in 1898, the band marched through the Windy City playing "Hot Time in the Old Town." That's when Louis Elbel decided something was lacking. He felt that the band needed "the right celebration song," which he soon provided. But the band was scooped on its own signature song. Before the 1899 football season began, John Philip Sousa gave "The Victors" its first public performance with his famous concert band.

The marching band didn't actually march onto the field until the 1903 season. Since then, the band and its "celebration song" have become an indispensable part of the Michigan football experience.

Hello, Mr. Yost

He first came to Michigan's attention in an 1897 game between the Wolverines and an underdog Ohio Wesleyan team. Fielding H. Yost was that club's coach, and when they could field only ten players, he suited up and played, too. Impressively, Yost's team held Michigan to a 0–0 tie.

Yost, though, didn't stick around. He went to Nebraska, then Kansas, then coached the 1900 season at Stanford; he won wherever he went. The problem was that with rare exceptions, full-time coaching jobs did not yet exist. The pay depended on whether the team made a profit, and many colleges gave a preference to their own alumni when it came to handing out those positions. When Stanford decided to go that route, Yost was out of pocket again.

Yost had graduated from West Virginia and had earned a law degree, and he knew he could always make a living as a lawyer. But Yost loved football too much to give it up, so he began the job hunt again.

Gustave Ferbert, an outstanding player in the 1890s, had coached Michigan to its first conference championship. He left for more stable work. His replacement, Bill Lea, was called back to his alma mater, Princeton, to coach. While Yost was looking for a new job, Michigan had decided it was time to hire a full-time coach.

Athletic Director Charles Baird heard that Yost was available, and he remembered that Ohio Wesleyan game. So in 1901, the man met the moment at Michigan. The deal was a professor's pay, $2,300 a year, plus room and board.

Yost couldn't get there fast enough. He was just 30 years old and so eager to start that he ran from the railroad station up the hill to campus. Anybody who didn't bring that same sense of urgency to the game could not play for Fielding H. Yost. His nickname, "Hurry Up," was no random designation.

From that day on, everything changed. This is when Michigan became Meee-chigan, which is how Yost liked to pronounce it. The undefeated season of 1898 had brought a bit of national attention. Center William Cunningham was named to the All-America team, becoming the first Michigan player so honored.

But Yost's vision was much bigger than that. Beginning in 1901, he moved Michigan to the very center of the football stage. The Wolverines became not only champions of the West but the preeminent college program in America, with four consecutive national titles.

> "Many have the will to win, but few have the will to prepare."
>
> **Fielding Yost**

Yost referred to the school in Ann Arbor as Meee-chigan, a pronunciation that Bob Ufer and other broadcasters would mimic in later years.

Everything that followed was built on the foundation that Yost had laid. He demanded academic integrity, and he insisted that the athletic campus become the finest possible. The rules allowed lots of leeway in recruiting in the early years, and Yost—trained as a lawyer—took advantage of the loopholes. In later years, however, he became an advocate for strict regulation.

Yost made sure that Michigan scheduled intersectional games to give the program wide national exposure. However, he also knew that the season would be a dud unless he beat the traditional rivals. In Yost's day, that meant Chicago, and in his first four years he went 4–0 against U-C. When the conference tried to negate him by limiting the number of outside games members could play, Yost felt Chicago's coach, Amos Alonzo Stagg, was behind it. Eventually, Yost took the team out of the Big Ten. The conference retaliated by refusing to allow any of its members to schedule Michigan. But Yost's caravan rolled on.

When it suited him, Yost returned to the Big Ten, and after 1921 he also served as Michigan's athletic director. He spent most of the next decade in the planning and construction of Michigan Stadium, and he decided to step down from coaching entirely after the 1923 season.

But not so fast. His successor, George Little, did the unpardonable. He not only lost a homecoming game, but he went down to Illinois for the dedication of the new stadium there and allowed Red Grange to run wild over the Wolverines in a 39–14 drubbing.

That was intolerable. Yost reclaimed the job in 1925 and finished 7–1. When the team went back to Illinois to play Grange again, the "Galloping Ghost" was held completely in check. Michigan won 3–0.

That was the only acceptable outcome for Fielding Yost.

During practices, Yost often began his sentences with "Hurry up." He'd say, "Hurry up and be the first man to line up. . . . Hurry up when given the ball for a gain. You must hurry or the opponents will be all over you in an instant."

Point-a-Minute Dynasty

No one ever had seen a football team like this. The players were faster than ponies. When opponents started to fade, the Wolverines were just getting started. Their plays were run with the precision of a machine. That was exactly it. Fielding Yost's players were machine-like in their execution. But instead of going a mile a minute like a crack express train, they scored a point a minute.

The 1902 team scored 644 points in 11 games—or 660 minutes. But that was with touchdowns counting only five points and some teams conceding defeat in the fourth quarter.

No one came within 21 points of Yost's 1901 team, and no one scored a point on them, either. Poor Buffalo was annihilated 128–0. Even good teams, teams that had beaten or tied Michigan the previous year, were wiped out. The Wolverines crushed Ohio State 21–0, Chicago 22–0, and Iowa 50–0.

In 1902, the Michigan Agricultural School, which

Below: Michigan broke more than just Stanford's spirit in the inaugural Rose Bowl game in 1902. Stanford guard William Roosevelt, cousin of President Theodore Roosevelt, broke his leg and ribs during the 49–0 Michigan rout.

OFFICIAL SCORES OF YESTERDAY.
Michigan **128** Buffalo **0**

Harvard	29	Carlisle	0
West Point	15	Williams	0
Princeton	4	Lafayette	0
Northwestern	17	Illinois	0
Indiana	11	Purdue	6
Pennsylvania	11	Chicago	0
Minnesota	16	Iowa	0
Yale	10	Columbia	5
Cornell	29	Oberlin	0
Brown	6	Holy Cross	0
Nebraska	17	Ames	0
Pennsylvania State	22	Gettysburg	0
Wisconsin	28	Kansas	0

would become Michigan State, went down to the worst defeat in its history, 119–0, and Iowa was throttled 107–0. In his first five seasons at Michigan, Yost's teams went 55–1–1 and won four straight national championships. During that 57-game span, 50 opponents were shut out. So it wasn't just an offensive machine that Yost built, but an impregnable defensive wall as well.

Michigan had fielded good teams in the past, but nothing like this. The College Football Hall of Fame calls them "the most devastating teams in history." Even the eastern writers, who would never concede any team was the match of Yale or Princeton, deigned to give Michigan the western half of the national title. "Yale was king of the conquered east and Michigan ruled the west," rhapsodized columnist Grantland Rice.

How did Yost do it? He brought extraordinary discipline to his practices. They were meticulously planned and run at top speed, with the coach yelling "hurry up" whenever the pace slackened. While other teams relied on brawn to win games, Yost was a master of deception and quickness. Everything Michigan did was run up-tempo. He believed in the quick kick, often punting on third down to get better field position. Of course, his offense was so efficient that he seldom was placed in a third-down situation.

Yost drilled in fundamentals, but he threw in a double reverse to beat Chicago one year. He also is credited with inventing the no-huddle offense and being the first coach

Left: Prior to 1901, the Wolverines had never approached anything as absurd as 100 points in a game. But with Fielding Yost's high-powered offense, all things were possible. Their average margin of victory in 1901 was 55–0.

Weeks, Shorts, Snow, Heston, Herrnstein

TACKLE-BACK-RIGHT PLAY.

FIRST TOURNAMENT OF ROSES GAME, MICHIGAN VS. STANFORD.
PASADENA, JANUARY 1, 1902.
— SCORE —
MICHIGAN 49   STANFORD 0

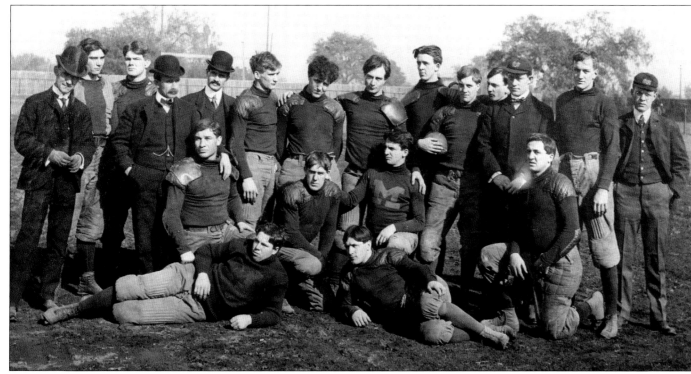

This unassuming bunch was the 1901 Michigan football team, perhaps the most dominant juggernaut in the history of college football. Fullback Neil Snow was the only Michigan player named to the All-America team.

to understand the potential of the forward pass. Notre Dame got the credit when the Irish used it to upset Army in 1913, but Yost had employed the pass to beat Minnesota three years earlier.

When Minnesota actually managed to tie Michigan, 6–6, in 1903, breaking a streak of 29 straight wins, the Gophers and their fans partied deep into the night. Holding the Point-a-Minute group even was regarded as an epic accomplishment. That game was also the start of the Little Brown Jug trophy. Michigan left its water container on the bench in the postgame confusion, and when Minnesota was asked to return it, the Wolverines were told to win it back. This was difficult because of scheduling restrictions, but six years later Yost took his team back to Minneapolis and pulled off a 15–6 win. They have played for the trophy ever since.

The streak finally ended with a 2–0 loss to Chicago in the final game of 1905—the only points Michigan gave up all year. But the personality of Yost and the Point-a-Minute teams had been stamped on college football forever.

The First Rose Bowl

Yost's first Point-a-Minute team was so good, it almost killed the Rose Bowl after its very first year. Following its undefeated season of 1901, Michigan was invited to Pasadena, California, by the Tournament of Roses committee to play the best team on the West Coast (the Pac-10 Conference had yet to be formed). The best team was Stanford, the very school that had told Yost to move along the previous year.

The committee members were looking to publicize Pasadena, then an obscure but sunny little town, with a national sporting event on New Year's Day. Attractions such as polo and greased pig catching hadn't worked, so they gave football a try.

Yost got his payback. With Michigan ahead 49–0 and eight minutes still to play, Stanford ran out of able-bodied men and conceded. The first Rose Bowl was so lopsided, in fact, that it took 14 years before they held a second one. Michigan didn't return until New Year's Day, 1948, when the result was exactly the same—a 49–0 walloping of Southern California.

Long before Nike, these men are busy making the official shoes of the Michigan football team.

Penn was the scourge of the Wolverines from 1906 to '08, beating U-M each year.

This postcard dates to 1907, when Michigan shut out its first five opponents before being whitewashed itself by Pennsylvania in the sixth and final game.

This stylish mug, from 1905, was shaped like a topless football. A Michigan pennant and football laces were also painted on this mug.

In a battle of unbeatens, Michigan defeated Minnesota 10–0 in the 1923 season finale to earn national championship recognition.

While U-M was named national champion by many organizations from 1901 through '04, other associations gave the title to eastern schools each year. For example, Parke Davis recognized Yale in both 1901 and '02.

The turkey wasn't the only one who "got it" on Thanksgiving Day, 1902. Minnesota (*right*) fell victim to the Wolverines, who won 23–6.

From 1911 to '31, Michigan's fight song wasn't "The Victors" but instead "Varsity," which the Michigan band still plays today.

Early-Day Stars

The Point-a-Minute teams were loaded with stars, but two shone a bit brighter than the rest. Halfback Willie Heston and center Germany Schulz rank among the greatest college football players of the 20th century's first half.

Heston was fast enough to beat the 1904 Olympic gold-medal winner in the 40-yard sprint—several times. Observers said that he used the straight arm like a bludgeon and carried tacklers hanging from his shoulders into the end zone. The story was that he could run straight at a brick wall and, just when everyone was braced for the collision, would find a way to shift around it.

"He could slice through an opening the width of my hand and pivot on a dime," said Schulz, who blocked for him in 1904. "He was a streak."

Many years later, Fielding Yost was asked whether Heston would have been so dominant playing in the era of the forward pass. "He'd have been better," Yost insisted. "You couldn't cover him. Next to [heavyweight champion] Gentleman Jim Corbett, he was the quickest man I ever saw."

Heston arrived in Ann Arbor with $2.65 in his pocket after Yost had invited him to play for Michigan. Heston already had played three years at San Jose Normal, and Yost had coached him there in 1900 when he wasn't otherwise coaching Stanford. Heston enrolled in law school at Michigan and played four more years. (Eligibility was a lot less formal back then.)

According to school records, he was credited with 72 touchdowns in his four years at Michigan. He stood 5'8", weighed 190 pounds, and ran the 100-yard dash in ten seconds flat. When Michigan went to the Rose Bowl in 1901, Yost used Heston as a decoy in goal-line situations. While fullback Neil Snow scored five touchdowns, Heston still ran for 170 yards.

Snow, like Heston, was on the All-America team of 1901. He also was a ten-letter man, earning eight letters in football and baseball and two letters in track. He was a conference high jump champion, and observers said he could have played in the major leagues. "No college ever developed a better all-around athlete," said Walter Camp, who picked the All-America squads.

But it was Schulz who had the biggest impact of them all. He not only was the first center to snap the ball one-handed for greater ease in blocking, but he

One of the fastest men in the world in the early 1900s, Willie Heston officially rushed for 72 touchdowns in his career—which remains a Michigan record.

> "He could slice through an opening the width of my hand and pivot on a dime. He was a streak."
>
> **Germany Schulz on Willie Heston**

Captain of the 1900 Michigan team, Neil Snow earned All-America honors as an end in 1901. In that season's Rose Bowl against Stanford, he scored five touchdowns—good enough to earn him induction into the Rose Bowl Hall of Fame.

Named to college football's All-Time Team in 1951, Germany Schulz was the first defensive player to drop off the line (thus becoming football's first linebacker). Schulz worked in a steel mill in the off-seasons to improve his strength.

The Greatest Arm on Earth

It took a humiliation to get Benny Friedman into the lineup. But once he was in, he never left. He was regarded as the greatest passer of the single-wing era, with a touch so sure that he could hit prize receiver Bennie Oosterbaan in full stride every time. The combination of "Benny to Bennie" was unstoppable during the 1920s.

Not until Illinois and Red Grange thrashed Michigan 39–14 in 1924 did Friedman get his chance. He came off the bench the following week to beat Wisconsin 21–0, and he went 17–3 over the rest of his career with the Wolverines. Yost said his performance in the 54–0 blowout of Navy in 1925 was the finest by a quarterback he had ever seen.

Benny Friedman

"The Old Man [Yost] told me to look over the defense, play for field position, and remember [P. T.] Barnum was right," Friedman said. "In other words, there's a sucker born every minute, and the quarterback's job was to find the opposing player who would bite at the critical time." No one was better at picking that patsy than Benny.

invented the position of linebacker on defense. Until he dropped off the line during the 1904 season, no one else had thought of it.

Schulz never told Yost what he intended to do, and the first time he pulled back the coach had a conniption. "If anyone gets by me, I'll move back into the line," said Schulz. No one did. Schulz simply reasoned that he could get to the hole faster than the ball carrier if he was unencumbered. He weighed almost 250 pounds, huge for the era, and could run like a halfback. And once he got his hands on a runner, the play was over. "Please, sir," an overmatched Oberlin player once told him. "If you are determined to be fierce, I'll get out of the way."

Yost always claimed that Schulz's greatest game was in a 29–0 loss to Penn in 1908, his senior year. With ten minutes left, the game was scoreless and Schulz was fighting off three blockers on every play to make tackles. Penn's game plan was to knock him out of the game, and when they finally succeeded they scored five straight touchdowns. Those were the only ten minutes Schulz missed in his entire career.

Fielding's Last Hurrah

For Fielding Yost, it was like the pursuit of the white whale. He could rack up one win after another by astronomical scores. But until he beat one of the top eastern teams, he knew that Michigan would never get the national recognition it deserved.

After the Western Conference adopted scheduling restrictions, the Wolverines left the conference in 1907. Yost felt compelled to go after the one achievement that had eluded him: beating eastern schools. Scheduling was hard, and in some seasons he could line up only six games. But among them was Penn, a national powerhouse.

Yost lost three straight to the Quakers, never scoring a point on them. Penn's national championship-bound team visited Ann Arbor in 1908 and mauled Michigan 29–0. But a year later, Yost finally broke through. He went to Philadelphia and whipped an unbeaten Penn team 12–6. Three years later, he beat Cornell, another of the mighty East Coast teams. The quest thus satisfied, he returned to the Big Ten in 1917.

None of Yost's later teams were quite as dominant as the Point-a-Minute group. His 1918 squad got some support as national champions, although it was a season frustratingly cut short by the great flu epidemic and travel restrictions imposed by World War I. Michigan won all five of its games but had to cancel several others. Most informal polls gave the title to Pittsburgh, even though the Panthers saw their 32-game unbeaten streak ended.

After a losing season in 1919, the only one ever for Yost, he roared into the '20s with another group of powerful teams. He was masterful at developing terrific

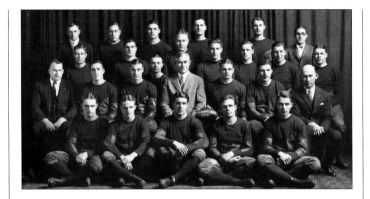

Michigan went 8–0 in 1923, yielding just 15 points all season, to win the conference and national championships. Here, the "champions" ball rests between the laps of coach Fielding Yost and captain Harry Kipke.

centers; three in a row—Ernie Vick, Jack Blott, and Robert Brown—were All-Americans. In 1923 undefeated Michigan broke through again. Captained by another great back, Harry Kipke (who specialized in "coffin corner" punts), this was Yost's sixth and final squad to win a national championship.

The Title That Blew Away

Yost ruefully claimed that 1925 was the national championship that got away. He said that that team, which he came back to lead after a one-year retirement, was his best ever. Its schedule was much stronger than the Point-a-Minute group, with tough Big Ten competition and a game with Navy.

The '25 Wolverines featured five All-Americans. Yost adapted his offensive thinking to the new passing game, and his defense shut out seven of its eight opponents. But Michigan missed out at the national title when Northwestern beat the Wolverines 3–2 at Chicago's Soldier Field.

That game was a disaster. A 55-mph wind blew in from Lake Michigan, and neither team could do anything. Northwestern gave up a safety rather than kick into the howling gale. That decision, along with a chip-shot field goal, sealed the game and doomed Michigan's perfect season.

The Fan Experience

Attending Michigan games was a rather leisurely experience in the early years. Aside from some of the more enthusiastic students, no one got too worked up. The team played on a stretch of grass at a fairground in the Burns Park area, about half a mile east of the present athletic complex. No tailgate parties were held, but many fans enjoyed a nice picnic. Attendance counts were haphazard, if taken at all. The press gave college football just a fraction of the coverage that it gave to baseball, boxing, and horseracing. If a really big game was coming up, chances are it would be moved off campus, to Detroit or Chicago. Once, Michigan even played indoors, at the Chicago Coliseum in 1896.

A new home ground, Regents Field, was built in 1893 for a whopping $8,000, but its stands could accommodate only a few hundred people. It was located on State Street, at the present site of Schembechler Hall. Temporary bleachers were installed for a few games, but even the Point-a-Minute teams rarely drew overflow crowds. The Wisconsin game of 1905 set an attendance record (18,000).

Yost knew that there was a lot more that could be done. The elements that make up so much of the Michigan tradition—the songs and the band, the cheerleaders and the winning teams—were already in place. So when Dexter Ferry donated 21 acres of land for a new field, just to the south and west of Regents Field, the team moved there in 1906. The capacity of Ferry Field was quickly expanded to 21,000 with a concrete grandstand.

Though this outfit (from 1908) might be a bit over the top, fans did dress up for Michigan football games in the early 1900s. Many women wore big hats, like this one, to Ferry Field.

Ann Arbor, Mich. The Block M at a game on Ferry Field, University of Michigan.

By the 1920s, sports were big business. Football fans were filling massive stadiums, and Yost—in his new role as athletic director—wanted Michigan to grow with the times. Ferry Field was enlarged to 45,000 seats, and attending a game in a raccoon coat while carrying a hip flask was the thing to do. The place sold out for big games with Illinois, Minnesota, and Ohio State. Starting in 1924, fans could hear Ty Tyson calling Wolverines games on the radio.

But an even bigger dream was in Yost's mind. Michigan's main rivals were opening stadiums that dwarfed U-M's aging facility. Yost proposed building the biggest college football stadium in the country to place Michigan in the vanguard of the new era. And he wanted it to happen soon.

Fans at Ferry Field hold up maize and blue pennants to form the Michigan block M. When football was moved to Michigan Stadium in 1927, Ferry Field was converted to an outdoor track and field facility, which is still in use today.

Michigan Magic

1927–1947

Fritz Crisler reawakens a dormant program and wins a championship with the most magical and imaginative offense ever seen in the Big Ten. Such stars as Tom Harmon and the "Mad Magicians" thrill Michigan fans and fill the long rows of seats in the Big House.

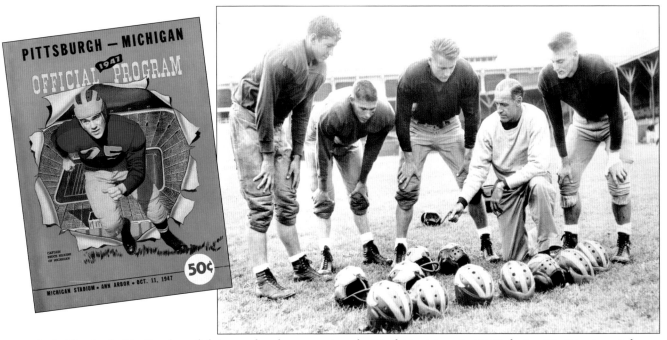

Left: *The lowly Pitt Panthers didn't stand a chance against the Mad Magicians in 1947, losing 69–0 in Ann Arbor.*
Right: *Fritz Crisler instructs team stars Bill Daley, Elroy Hirsch, Paul White, and Bob Wiese (left to right) during the team's 8–1 campaign in 1943. Michigan outscored its opponents 302–73 and finished No. 3 in the AP poll.*

A national sensation, Tom Harmon—"Old 98"—averaged 6.8 yards per carry in 1939 and became Michigan's first Heisman Trophy winner in 1940.

The Big House

Maybe it was a sentimental gesture by Fielding Yost. The opponent he selected for the first game at Michigan Stadium was Ohio Wesleyan, the same school he had coached 30 years before in his very first game in Ann Arbor. A grand total of 17,483 people showed up this time.

Yost knew that the massive 84,401-seat stadium still had some kinks that needed to be addressed. So the opener was billed as a shakedown cruise, and the "official" opening didn't come until the third home game of the 1927 season. The place sold out that day, and Ohio State obligingly went down in defeat, 21–0.

If Yost was in a jubilant mood, no one could blame him. It had been a long, tough haul to get this stadium built. It called for every ounce of persuasion, politicking, and prestige at his disposal. He had to overcome construction problems, financing problems, and the active disapproval of the university faculty.

But this was Fielding H. Yost. He went behind the scenes to line up support from politicians and influential university alumni. He urged the Detroit Fire Department

All tickets were sold for the Michigan Stadium dedication game, played on October 22, 1927. The $3 admission fee was the equivalent of $35 in today's money.

to bring in pumpers when groundwater threatened to flood the site, and then he built the university golf course across the road so that the water could be diverted and used there. When the approved plan was 10,000 seats shy of the size he wanted, he arranged for 10,000 "temporary" seats to be placed in the upper concourse. Somehow, they remained in place for the next 22 years.

The total land acquisition and construction cost was $1.1 million, while the time from groundbreaking to opening took 13 months. Michigan Stadium was the largest college-owned facility in America. The Big House (as it

On October 26, 1941, 84,658 fans—the biggest Michigan Stadium crowd in 12 years—watched the Wolverines lose a 7–0 heartbreaker to Minnesota.

would become known decades later) was open for business.

Yost and his architect, Bernard Green, had studied stadium configurations from around the world and into antiquity. They used the Yale Bowl as a model, but instead of a true oval they set the seats between the goal lines directly parallel to the field for a more intimate feeling.

Unfortunately, the stadium turned out to be far too big. Yost did not foresee the Great Depression and World War II, two of the most effective attendance suppressants in history. The stadium sold out just a handful of times in its first 19 years. The original design allowed for an expansion to more than 100,000 seats, but that would have to wait until 1956.

Yost soon realized he had a big problem. He scheduled doubleheaders to start the season from 1929 to 1931. They didn't draw. He added electronic scoreboards in 1930, and he posted the official time so that everyone could see. Those didn't have much of an impact, either. Some years, even the biggest crowd of the season filled only half the stadium. Moreover, not a penny was paid back on the construction bonds during most of the 1930s.

What made it even worse was that Michigan football went into eclipse. In the 27 seasons after Yost arrived in 1901, the Wolverines had one losing season. In the 11 years after the Big House opened, they had three of them. This wasn't good for business.

> **"People looked at that hole in the ground and said, 'Oh, man, Yost is off his rocker.'"**
>
> **Kip Taylor, an end on Michigan's 1927 team**

Even Ohio Wesleyan beat them, for heaven's sake, in the 1928 home opener. Yost canned his hand-picked successor, Tad Wieman, after that debacle of a season (3–4–1) and brought in Harry Kipke, who had starred on the 1923 national champions.

Always a revered figure on the Michigan campus, Yost now began hearing accusations that he was a meddler who couldn't keep his hands off the program that he had elevated to national prominence. The empty seats at the stadium haunted him, and he would not see it filled regularly during his lifetime.

But the facility that has not drawn a crowd of less than 100,000 since 1975 is a monument to Yost's genius as a coach and his vision as a builder. "The hole that Yost dug," as longtime play-by-play announcer Bob Ufer liked to describe it, has paid for itself many times over.

The Michigan Daily gave big play to the stadium's official opening in 1927. Wrote sports editor Herbert E. Vedder: "Just a few moments before 3 o'clock the Michigan eleven raced onto the field amid a deafening roar of cheering."

Four Seasons, One Loss

It was said that Harry Kipke could punt a football 50 yards onto a folded sweatshirt. That kind of delicate touch was useful when he took over as Michigan's head coach in 1929. He was expected to fashion a quick return to greatness for a struggling program while his former coach, Fielding Yost, looked on with a critical eye.

Kipke is remembered now as the interval between Yost and Fritz Crisler. Buildings are named for them, but just a short street leading into a stadium parking lot was dedicated to Kipke. Yet his record can stand with anyone—at least for the first half of his career. He led Michigan to four straight conference championships and back-to-back national titles in 1932–33.

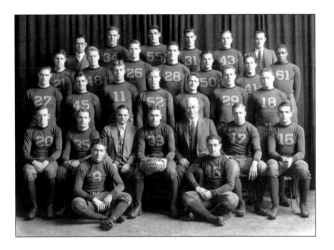

Halfback/quarterback Stan Fay (holding ball) captained the undefeated 1933 team. Future U.S. president Gerald Ford (No. 48) was a backup lineman.

Kipke said that his coaching scheme consisted of "a punt, a pass, and a prayer." He was the first to utter the chestnut "a great defense is a great offense." Kipke is also the only Michigan head coach to be hired from Michigan State, and when he returned to Ann Arbor it took him less than two years to get things rolling.

From 1930 through 1933, he compiled a record of 31–1–3. While the Depression tightened its coils around Michigan's automotive industry, Kipke's winning teams pulled customers into the Big House. A few commentators have even credited him with saving a program that had been overextended by Yost's ambitious building plans.

Kipke used the economy as an ally. He was connected in political and business circles, and he became close friends with Harry Bennett—the right-hand man of Henry Ford. Michigan players could count on a summer job at Ford, and that proved to be a powerful recruiting tool.

Kipke's 1932 team shut out six of eight opponents, and only a scoreless tie with Minnesota marred the 1933 record. However, his next four teams went 10–22, the worst stretch in Michigan football history. After 1937, Kipke was history, too.

A Triple Threat

The Heisman Trophy did not yet exist in 1932; otherwise, quarterback Harry Newman almost certainly would have won it. He did accept the Douglas Fairbanks Trophy, which went to the season's best player.

Harry Newman

Newman had a direct hand in 57 of the 83 points Michigan scored in the Big Ten in 1932, as the Wolverines went undefeated and won the national championship. His soaring field goal that beat Minnesota 3–0 in the tense season finale was called Newman's wiliest play of the year by *Time* magazine. A true triple threat out of the single wing, Newman was regarded as the Big Ten's best passer since Benny Friedman.

Newman's promising pro career with the New York Giants was cut short by injuries, although he did hold the distinction of throwing the first touchdown pass in an NFL championship game, as a rookie in 1933.

Buckeye Fever

It was always a big date on the calendar, although maybe not in the same category as Illinois or Minnesota. ("We played them for blood," recalled Benny Friedman.) But Ohio State was one of the sure draws at Michigan Stadium, and when the Horseshoe opened in Columbus in 1922 Michigan was a perennial sellout there, too. It was a pretty one-sided rivalry, though. When the Wolverines blanked the Buckeyes in 1933 on the way to their fourth straight Big Ten title, they improved their record against OSU to 22–6–2.

Then two things happened: Francis Schmidt arrived to coach the Bucks, and the Ohio State game was moved to the last slot on the schedule. For many years, that spot had been taken by Minnesota. But in 1935 and after, Michigan vs. Ohio State was (with just one exception) the season finale. As the years went by, the game's importance was magnified above all others.

Much of that was the work of Schmidt, who had arrived from the Southwest Conference knowing that he had one big job: Beat Michigan. He did that astonishingly well. In his first four years in Columbus (1934–37), he clobbered the Wolverines by an aggregate score of 114–0. Few teams had ever manhandled Michigan so consistently and so rudely.

Schmidt played a wide-open kind of football that the press labeled razzle-dazzle. He loved to run up the score, too, earning the nickname "Close the Gates of Mercy." He also uttered a phrase that would become a cliché when he

said that Michigan players "put on their pants one leg at a time like everyone else." The Ohio State faithful loved it, and to this day Buckeyes who play on a team that beats Michigan receive tiny gold pants as a token.

When the charm wore off and Fritz Crisler beat OSU three times in a row, the gates of mercy in Columbus slammed shut in Schmidt's face, too. From that point on, a coach at either school who failed to win this game was on the hot seat, no matter what else he did. This was the litmus test.

It was the main reason Fritz Crisler and Bo Schembechler were brought to Ann Arbor, and it was certainly the reason Paul Brown, Woody Hayes, and Jim Tressel got the chance to win national titles at OSU. It remains the greatest rivalry in all American athletics.

After 1934, the Ohio State game became the last on Michigan's schedule for the rest of the century (and beyond). The only exception was in 1942, when Michigan played Iowa in the finale.

Even during the Depression and World War II, 60,000 to 70,000 fans packed The Horseshoe in Columbus to indulge in the interstate rivalry.

Georgia Tech agreed to play Michigan in 1934 only if U-M barred African American Willis Ward from the game. Michigan acceded to the demand. The Wolverines' 9-2 win was their only victory of the year.

The Wolverines' 85 points in the 1939 Chicago game are the most they have scored in the last hundred-plus years (since 1904).

This etching of an early-day game at Michigan Stadium shows that the place was just as packed, and the fans were just as rabid, as during contemporary Michigan games.

The University of Chicago dumped its football program after the 1939 season, in part because of its humiliating loss to Michigan that October.

In September 1940, Michigan players became the first collegians to fly cross-country for a football game. Players under 21 needed their parents' permission for the flight to California; all consented.

Even the Buffalo Courier-Express played up the 1930 Michigan-Ohio State game. On a bitterly cold October afternoon, U-M won 13–0.

Ticket prices for Michigan games dropped during the Depression, including those for this 1934 contest. Only 21,963 showed up to see U-M lose to Wisconsin, 10–0.

The Presidential Center

When a man achieves prominence in later life, his early-day accomplishments are sometimes exaggerated. So it was with Gerald Ford, the 38th president of the United States and starting center on the 1934 Michigan football team.

After his senior season in 1934, Ford was offered $200 a game to play for the Detroit Lions. However, he turned down the offer in order to coach football (as an assistant) and attend law school at Yale.

Despite the mythology, Ford was never mentioned on any All-America team, nor was he ever Michigan's captain. He was not a starter in a single game during the championship seasons of 1932 and 1933, although he did letter. In his one year as a regular, Michigan suffered through a 1–7 campaign.

Having said that, though, it should also be mentioned that assistant coach Bennie Oosterbaan called his performance during that futile season one of the most courageous he had ever seen, and Ford was voted the team's MVP. He remained an avid Michigan fan. After becoming president in 1974, he sometimes requested that "The Victors" be played at official functions instead of "Hail to the Chief."

One of Ford's closest friends on that team was end Willis Ward, an outstanding track and field star who once beat Olympian Jesse Owens in the 60-yard dash. Ward was the first African American to start for Michigan in the 20th century, and he was the central figure in one of the most dismal incidents in the school's history.

Georgia Tech sent word that it would not honor its commitment to play at Michigan in 1934 if Ward was allowed to compete. Michigan athletic director Fielding

Willis Ward not only was banned from the 1934 game, but he wasn't allowed to watch from the Michigan Stadium bench or press box. He did have support: Before the game, a thousand Michigan students signed a petition demanding that he play.

Yost, who had never permitted a black player on teams he coached, acceded to the demand (although coach Harry Kipke wanted him to play). When Ward was told the news, he wanted to quit the team. In addition, Ford threatened to lead a boycott by several other players. But Kipke convinced them that such a response would ruin the chances of other black athletes playing at Michigan in the future. Ward stayed away from the stadium and word was put out that he had the flu.

Michigan took the game 9–2 for its only win of the year, but the incident demoralized the team. No other southern school was invited to the Big House for 19 years, nor did the Wolverines travel to a southern state until 1965.

Ford and Ward remained friends for the rest of their lives. In fact, when Ward—who became an attorney and a judge—ran for Congress in Detroit as a Republican, Ford took time to campaign for him.

The Genius of Crisler

The nickname was a joke made by his college coach, Amos Alonzo Stagg. He said that young Herbert Crisler looked so bad in practice that he would name him after the brilliant violinist Fritz Kreisler, "for reasons of contrast."

Fritz Crisler eventually became a fairly good end at the University of Chicago. But as a coach, he was touched with the genius of his namesake. He took Michigan into the modern era and initiated the second great dynasty in the school's football history, going 71–16–3 in his ten seasons.

When he was hired from Princeton before the 1938 season, it was not a popular choice. Crisler was, after all, not a Michigan man but a product of its ancient rival, Stagg's Chicago. And while Crisler had led Princeton to two undefeated seasons in his six years there, that competition simply did not measure up to the Big Ten.

Crisler shares a smile with George Ceithaml, the quarterback and captain of the 1942 Wolverines.

But Crisler took a Michigan program that hadn't won in four years and immediately brought it back to national prominence. Of course, it helped that his first sophomore class included Tom Harmon and Forest Evashevski, and he also inherited a fast, dynamic line anchored by guard Ralph Heikkinen.

Crisler's players swore that they were better prepared than the opposition. Moreover, he seemed to have a sixth sense about an adjustment that could win a game. Crisler switched blocking assignments on punt returns against Illinois in 1947, and it resulted in a 74-yard touchdown—the margin of victory in the 14–7 game. "What's the score?" he would ask his players when they had a big lead. The only correct answer, no matter what it said on the scoreboard, was 0–0.

But Crisler's greatest innovation was two-platoon football. He said it was brought on by desperation when playing a veteran, unbeaten Army team in 1945. Michigan was outmanned and outgunned, but by shuttling separate offensive and defensive units onto the field, he held Army close most of the game before losing 28–7. Crisler had found a loophole in wartime college football rules that allowed substitutions "at any time" instead of once a quarter. In so doing, he changed the game forever.

A Distinct Look

The winged helmet gives Michigan one of the most readily identifiable looks in sports. That was the whole idea. Fritz Crisler wanted to install a quick-strike aerial attack in 1938. It depended on his passer being able to spot downfield receivers in a hurry, and Crisler reasoned that a distinctive helmet would provide the quarterback with a fast visual clue.

Until that time, Michigan, like all teams, wore basic black headgear, but Crisler's innovation is now part of football couture. He also was a great believer in tear-away jerseys, especially after he lost a game at Princeton when one of his backs was dragged down by the shirt. He featured the tear-aways at Michigan, which proved to be especially advantageous for the shifty running of Tom Harmon.

Old 98

When he trotted off the field near the end of the 1940 Ohio State game, the capacity crowd gave him a standing ovation. Several spectators ran out of the stands to touch him or try and get a piece of his jersey. The astonishing thing was that the game was played in Columbus.

The crowd had just watched Tom Harmon destroy their Buckeyes 40–0. He had run for three touchdowns and passed for two more. The fans knew they had just witnessed one of the greatest performances in college football history. In fact, the debate after Harmon's final game was whether he was the best player in the history of Michigan . . . or the Big Ten . . . or all of college football.

> "There is no comparing Tom Harmon and Red Grange. Grange was a great ball carrier while Harmon can do anything."
>
> **Fritz Crisler**

As heroes go, he looked the part. When he appeared on the cover of *Life* magazine two weeks before the OSU game, behind the simple headline "Michigan's Great Harmon," it could have been a still photo from every football movie ever made. Harmon, in fact, married a movie star, Elyse Knox, and their son, Mark, went on to an acting career—after starring as a quarterback at UCLA.

Actually, Harmon made his first big splash in California during the 1940 game at Berkeley. He returned the opening kickoff 95 yards for one touchdown, brought back a punt 70 yards for a second, and finished with 131 yards rushing. Those spectators rushed the field, too, although one of them came on prematurely in an attempt to tackle him.

Coach Fritz Crisler and star Tom Harmon display the halfback's torn jersey after one of his many brilliant games. Harmon's No. 98 is one of five numbers retired by the Michigan football program.

Harmon played only an eight-game schedule, and most of his records were eventually erased. So while he averaged more than 100 yards a game rushing and another 63 as a passer, the totals are modest by contemporary standards.

However, he could dominate a game in every aspect—punting, returning kicks, and even intercepting passes. Although his playing time was limited during his sophomore season, he still scored 33 touchdowns in his career, passed for 16 more, and added 39 more points with his foot. He was Michigan's first Heisman Trophy winner, and his uniform number, 98, was retired.

Harmon always gave Crisler the credit for turning him into a star. But his coach said that all he ever did was make sure Harmon had a football to run with. Injuries he suffered while bailing out of two airplanes during World War II cut short his pro career, but the cheering never ended for this legendary football hero.

Fritz's Biggest Games

It didn't take long for Fritz Crisler to demonstrate that Michigan was back. He blanked Michigan State 14–0 in the 1938 opener, the first time in five dreary years that the Wolverines had topped the Spartans. Just as encouraging, a crowd of 73,589—the biggest since 1933—turned out to see what the new coach could do.

During Michigan's decline, the Associated Press had instituted its weekly poll. Michigan made its first appearance there after week three in 1938, at No. 12. For the rest of Crisler's coaching tenure, Michigan would finish out of the rankings just four weeks and would place in the top ten for eight straight years.

Crisler mangled his alma mater, Chicago, 85–0 in 1939, one of the events that persuaded the school to drop intercollegiate competition altogether. The atom bomb would soon be developed under the stands of its deserted stadium.

The 40–0 evisceration of Ohio State in Columbus in 1940 had a less significant aftermath. But it did result in the Buckeyes pulling Paul Brown out of the high school coaching ranks and launching his historic college and pro career.

No matter what else he did, though, Crisler could not get past Minnesota. He lost to the Gophers five straight times, twice by 7–6 scores, defeats that sometimes cost Michigan the Big Ten championship. It was especially annoying because Minnesota had been his first head coaching job. But after he finally broke through, beating an

11th-ranked Minnesota team 49–6 in 1943, he never lost to them again.

Crisler placed his 32–20 triumph over Notre Dame in 1942 as the most emotional of his career, along with the 49–0 walloping of Southern California in the 1948 Rose Bowl. "A fan pointed out to me," Crisler joked, "it was the same score as the 1902 win over Stanford. So we hadn't made much progress in 46 years."

Paul Kromer runs to pay dirt during Michigan's 85–0 shellacking of Chicago in 1939. Tom Harmon ran for two TDs, threw for two, and kicked a field goal.

Flying to California

Games on the Pacific Coast are such a normal part of sports today that it's hard to imagine what a stir Crisler caused with Michigan's 1940 trip to play California. He put the Wolverines on three DC-3s, marking the first time any college team had flown across the country.

It wasn't the smoothest voyage. The planes made three refueling stops, and the journey took two days. But it beat the train, which was how eastern teams got to the Rose Bowl, and it opened up a new world of intersectional scheduling. The long flight didn't seem to hurt the team, either, as it rolled over Cal 41–0.

Because of wartime travel restrictions, Michigan couldn't repeat the trip until 1949, when it flew west to play Stanford. But it had blazed a path in the sky.

LIFE

MICHIGAN'S GREAT HARMON

NOVEMBER 11, 1940 **10** CENTS
YEARLY SUBSCRIPTION $4.50

Life on Tom Harmon: "His pile-driving legs grind his way through the line.... His speed leaves opponents far behind."

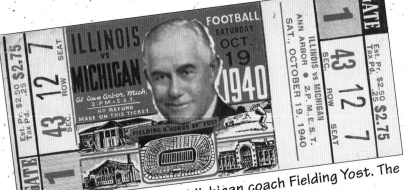

Tom Harmon and actress Anita Louise (*both pictured*) costarred in the 1941 film *Harmon of Michigan*. Harmon's wife, Elyse Knox, and three children all were actors.

This ticket honors former Michigan coach Fielding Yost. The 69-year-old legend celebrated U-M's 28–0 rout that day.

OFFICIAL PROGRAM

DYCHE STADIUM · EVANSTON

NORTHWESTERN *versus* MICHIGAN
OCTOBER 2, 1943
AFTER READING THIS PROGRAM MAIL IT TO A MAN IN SERVICE

This program illustrates how football and the war were intertwined in 1943. Two weeks earlier, Michigan faced Camp Grant, an Army training base.

Michigan football results have always made Page 1 of *The Michigan Daily*, even during World War II.

The Michigan Daily

VOL. LIII No. 27

ANN ARBOR, MICHIGAN, SUNDAY, NOV. 15, 1942

Weather
Warmer

PRICE FIVE CENTS

Allies Advance For Showdown In Africa
Varsity Routs Tough Notre Dame, 32-20

U.S. Warships Battle Japs in Solomons

Both Sides Suffering Losses in First Big Naval Engagement in Area Since Oct. 28

British Troops Chase Rommel

British artillerymen in Egypt advance as the Allied forces push Rommel back and out of Egypt. In the background infantry can be seen leading the attack which is now pushing past Tobruk.

Position of Vanguard Unknown

Reports Say Troops Cross Border 80 Miles From City of Tunis

Left: After the war, Tom Harmon played two seasons in the NFL. In 1947 his Los Angeles Rams faced the Lions in Detroit, inspiring Frank Williams of the *Detroit Free Press* to draw this collage. *Right:* Nearly 63,000 fans packed Yankee Stadium to see the Army juggernaut beat Michigan 28–7 in 1945.

FIFTY CENTS

ARMY ★ MICHIGAN

OCTOBER · 13 · 1945 · YANKEE STADIUM

Stars of the '40s

Bob Chappuis played halfback on the 1942 Michigan team and surely would have been a starter on the Big Ten champions the following season. Except that World War II got in the way.

Chappuis went into the Army Air Force instead, and while flying a mission over northern Italy in early 1945, his plane was shot down. He had to parachute behind German lines and was hidden by a family of partisans. When the boyfriend of one of the daughters threatened to turn him in, he was told that Chappuis would shoot the entire family if that happened. It was a bluff, but it saved his life until he could be rescued.

Forged by that experience, Chappuis returned to Michigan two years after his class would have graduated and developed into one of the greatest triple-threat halfbacks in school history. Chappuis was mentioned in the same breath as Tom Harmon, and as a passer he fired 24 touchdown passes in his career. In the 1948 Rose Bowl, he amassed 279 yards of total offense. He finished second in the Heisman voting that year and ended up on the cover of *Time* magazine.

Bob Chappuis was most deadly as a passer in 1947. He averaged 20.3 yards per completion and fired 13 touchdown strikes.

Bob Westfall, who played fullback in the Harmon backfield, emerged as a leader on his own after the great star departed following the 1940 season. In what was supposed to be a down year, Westfall captained a team that lost just one time. Crisler called him the best of the spinning fullbacks at Michigan, even though he weighed less than 180 pounds.

Because of wartime training programs, several great players from other schools wound up in Ann Arbor, and they keyed the 1943 conference champions. Bill Daley arrived from Minnesota and scored nine touchdowns while averaging 6.8 yards a carry. The halfback on that squad was Wisconsin's Elroy Hirsch. Already nicknamed "Crazy Legs," he was developing the pass-catching skills that would allow him to achieve stardom with the Los Angeles Rams. *Time* called them the "dream backfield."

A hard-driving fullback, Bob Westfall earned All-America honors for the Wolverines in 1941, when he led the Big Ten in scoring.

Elroy Hirsch was the first U-M athlete to letter in four sports in the same school year: football, baseball, basketball, and track.

The entire left side of the starting line, as well as center Fred Negus (a Wisconsin transfer), were also playing their only season at Michigan. But right tackle Merv Pregulman may have been the most versatile of them all. He shifted over from guard and center, where he had started for Michigan during the previous two seasons, to make room for the imports on other parts of the line. He was named to several All-America teams in recognition of his stellar adaptability.

When Crisler fully installed the two-platoon system, Marine Corps vet Elmer Madar was an anomaly. The rugged end was one of just two starters the coach trusted to play on both offense and defense. The converted quarterback made several All-America teams in 1946.

Another combat veteran among the 1947 Wolverines (70 percent of whom were attending college on the government under the GI Bill) was Chalmers "Bump" Elliott. He had been on the Purdue team that had tied Michigan for the Big Ten championship in 1943 before going off

Alvin and the Wisterts

First came Whitey. Then there was Ox and finally Moose. They were the Wistert brothers—better known as Francis, Albert, and Alvin, respectively. Beginning in 1931 and ending in 1949, they all played tackle at Michigan on a total of four national championship teams. In addition, they all wore No. 11 and they all were All-Americans.

"To have three brothers with the same basic drive and the God-given talent that it takes is amazing," said Albert in a 1969 interview. Also amazing is that none of the Wisterts, who came from Chicago, played high school football, reflecting Whitey's belief that "it will burn you out."

Alvin Wistert

Most amazing of all is that Alvin didn't play his first game for Michigan until he was 31, after serving with the Marines and spending a year with the Boston University team. He was the oldest man ever to play football for Michigan. Appropriately, he was elected captain of the 1949 team.

to war. Like Madar, he came back to play both ways in Crisler's system. He rushed for eight touchdowns from his right halfback slot, and his 74-yard punt return helped Michigan defeat Illinois 14–7. Elliott's running, teamed with the passing of Chappuis, made an unstoppable combination.

Approaching Greatness

The world was returning to normal in 1946. The war was over, fans were hungry for new heroes, and the college game was humming again. While some schools (including Michigan State) had to drop football during the war years and the manpower at many others was severely depleted, Fritz Crisler kept Michigan competitive. It helped that the campus was a military training facility and that stars from other schools were assigned there. From 1942 to 1945, Michigan went 30–9, always finishing among the top ten in the AP poll.

Crisler didn't back down from the toughies, either. Three of his losses were to national champions—Notre Dame, Ohio State, and Army—and two others were to star-studded service teams. The 1942 game with the Irish was the first time the teams met in 33 years, and Crisler wasn't especially happy about it. It was scheduled the week before the Ohio State game, for one thing. In addition, like many coaches of that era, he thought that scheduling Notre Dame caused divided loyalties among Catholic fans. It's how attitudes were back then.

In 1942 the Wolverines hammered the Irish 32–20. But Crisler claimed that the team lost to OSU the following week because it had nothing left emotionally. When they met the Irish again in 1943, it was the first game ever played between teams ranked first and second in the polls. It was carried on a national radio hookup, and a Michigan Stadium-record 86,408 arrived despite gas rationing and

Neither Michigan nor Notre Dame was thrilled about their scheduled meeting in 1942. The Irish were coming off an emotional game against Army at Yankee Stadium, and Michigan was depleted the next week against Ohio State.

other restrictions. Notre Dame romped 35–12, becoming the only team to score more than one touchdown against Michigan that year. Crisler later admitted that he didn't like Notre Dame coach Frank Leahy. The feeling was mutual, and the schools didn't play again for 35 years.

That 1943 team gave Crisler his first Big Ten championship. The Wolverines won 15 total games in 1944 and '45, and they remained strong in 1946. Crisler put together a young, tough, star-studded team. Many of his players had been shaped by their experiences in the war. They still couldn't get past Army, losing 20–13 to another undefeated Cadet team, but they did hold the great duo of Glenn Davis and Doc Blanchard in check. An interception on a tipped pass also meant a 13–9 loss to Illinois and missing out on the first game of the Big Ten's new contract with the Rose Bowl.

But the best was yet to come.

Army halfback Doc Blanchard weaves through the Michigan defense in their 1945 matchup in New York. Though the Wolverines lost 28–7, they were one of only two teams to lose by fewer than 32 points against the mighty Cadets that year.

The Mad Magicians

It was hard to tell if Fritz Crisler was joking when he said, "If you want to be sensational, bounce the ball, turn a somersault, then pick it up and run."

Crisler's undefeated 1947 team did everything with a football except turn it into a rabbit. No one had ever seen a team on which the ball was liable to end up in anyone's hands at any time. These Michigan men were called the "Mad Magicians," and were the greatest show in the game.

The nickname was cute, but unless you saw them play you couldn't really appreciate what they did. Members of the team who watched game films swore that they didn't know who had the ball half the time. Even Crisler would sometimes lose track of it from the sidelines.

Crisler's offensive philosophy was always based on deception—feinting at one point and hitting at another. His teams usually were outweighed by their opponents. In fact, the only team that gave them a real scare in 1947 was Minnesota, whose massive defense kept disrupting plays before the magic could begin. But Michigan found a way to win, 13–6.

All the plays out of the single wing went through the great spinning fullback, Jack Weisenburger. From there it could be a reverse, a buck lateral, a spin to the halfback or circling end, or a quick hitter. And the plays were run out of seven different formations. While other teams were switching to the T formation, Crisler's supposedly antiquated single wing was rewriting the book on offense.

Crisler took advantage of the two-platoon system. Only one or two men played both ways, as Michigan simply overwhelmed its opponents with fresh bodies. The

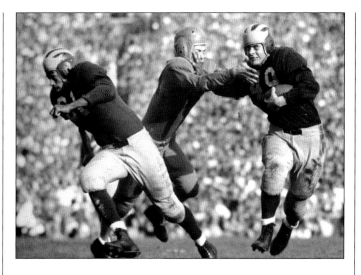

During their perfect 1947 season, Michigan gutted out a 13–6, comeback victory over a tough Minnesota team (pictured) and a 14–7 win over Illinois. Every other game was a blowout.

1947 team shut out half its opponents, winning by an average of 34 points. After a 21–0 pasting of Ohio State, it was on to the Rose Bowl.

Michigan 49, USC 0

Southern California was hardly a patsy. It had gone through an untarnished conference schedule in 1947, lost only to unbeaten Notre Dame, and was ranked No. 8 in the country in the final AP poll. Michigan had finished second, behind only the Irish.

But after U-M beat USC 49–0 in the Rose Bowl, the AP took an unprecedented step and held a postseason poll. Michigan was the victor. Notre Dame, which did not participate in bowl games and had beaten USC 38–7, fell to second.

The outcry among Irish partisans was so great that the AP backed off from its second poll and declared Notre Dame the "official" national champion. In Ann Arbor, however, 1947 has gone down as another title year for the Wolverines. Crisler, in his final year as coach, always regarded it to be as official as any other in Michigan history.

This trading card honors Joe Ponsetto, who in 1943 became the first freshman to start at quarterback for Michigan. A year later, he was named All-Big Ten.

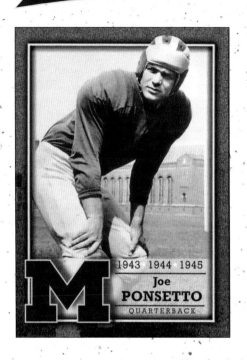

1943 · 1944 · 1945

Joe
PONSETTO
QUARTERBACK

Despite a wet and muddy field, the Michigan offense amassed 449 yards en route to a 21–0 washout of Ohio State in 1947.

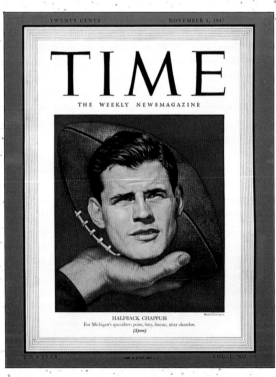

TWENTY CENTS   NOVEMBER 3, 1947

TIME
THE WEEKLY NEWSMAGAZINE

HALFBACK CHAPPUIS
For Michigan's specialists: poise, fury, finesse, utter abandon.
(Sport)

The words on the bottom of this *Time* cover summed up the style of Bob Chappuis and the rest of the Michigan backfield: "poise, fury, finesse, utter abandon." U-M was halfway to a 10–0 season in 1947 when this issue hit the stands.

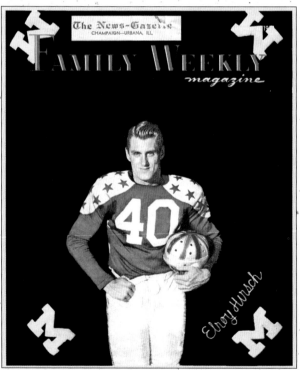

The News-Gazette
CHAMPAIGN-URBANA, ILL.

FAMILY WEEKLY
magazine

40

Elroy Hirsch

Sportswriter Francis Powers was the first to call Elroy Hirsch "Crazy Legs," claiming that his legs gyrated "in six different directions."

Bob Chappuis earned the 1948 Rose Bowl MVP Award after rushing for 91 yards, throwing for 188, and tossing two touchdown passes.

The Wolverines' triumph in the 1948 Rose Bowl was so resounding that they leapfrogged Notre Dame to the No. 1 spot in AP's first-ever post-bowl poll.

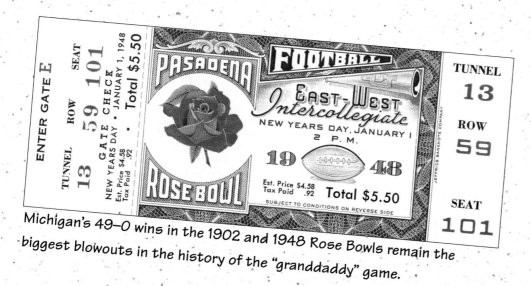

Michigan's 49–0 wins in the 1902 and 1948 Rose Bowls remain the biggest blowouts in the history of the "granddaddy" game.

Fritz Crisler and Bennie Ooosterbaan, the Wolverines' coaches from 1938 to '58, autographed this football for a lucky Michigan fan.

From Bennie to Bump

1948–1968

In 1948, Bennie Oosterbaan's first season as coach, Michigan runs the table en route to the national championship. The Wolverines struggle over the next two decades, but they field superstar players, exceed 100,000 in attendance for the first time, and wage memorable battles—including the most bizarre game in Michigan history.

Players hoist Bennie Oosterbaan on their shoulders at the conclusion of the 1958 season. The game marked the end of his 34 years at U-M as a player, assistant coach, and head coach.

The Michigan offense displays its many weapons in this well-choreographed photo shoot from 1949. The Wolverines extended their winning streak to 25 games that season.

Bennie in Charge

Bennie Oosterbaan was more accustomed to receiving a pass than a handoff. But he handled both with aplomb. Teaming with quarterback Benny Friedman, he gave the Wolverines the most feared passing attack in the country in 1925 and 1926—and even threw two TD passes himself in one game on the end-around play.

After 20 seasons as an assistant coach, he was handed the top job when Fritz Crisler stepped aside after the 1947 season to become full-time athletic director. The team he inherited was an undefeated, unstoppable force, and Oosterbaan led it to a second consecutive national championship.

For 34 years as a player, assistant, and head coach, Oosterbaan was directly involved in Michigan football—a run exceeded only by Fielding Yost. He was a three-time All-American, becoming the first Michigan player ever to achieve such a distinction. (Anthony Carter was the second.) He also led the Big Ten in scoring as a forward on the basketball squad. The world was open to him when he graduated in 1928. He had offers to play professional football and baseball. But his heart was in Ann Arbor, and he never left.

In his coaching career, however, the successes never quite seemed to compensate for the disappointments. Oosterbaan grabbed three straight conference championships and a Rose Bowl berth in his first three years. Then he never won a conference title again. After 1950, when the last of Crisler's players graduated, his record against Michigan State was 2–5–1; against Ohio State, 3–5. The 1955 team, led by Ron Kramer, was ranked No. 1 in the

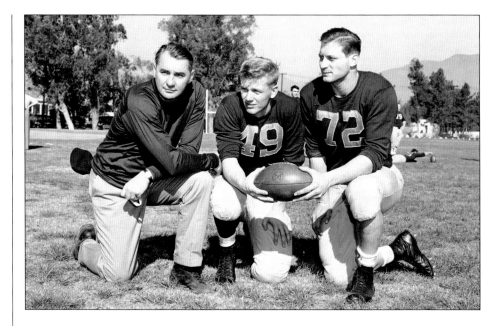

country for a few weeks but faltered badly down the stretch and finished third in the Big Ten.

The energy seemed to have fizzled out of the Michigan program. After the sparkle of the Crisler years, it was a severe letdown. Oosterbaan's critics said that his teams lacked the discipline, drive, and flair of his predecessor. Only in a few seasons did they rise to a level above lackluster. He was just too nice, they insisted, or maybe he had put in too many years.

Finally, alumni unhappiness led him to retire after a 1958 campaign in which he had posted a 2–6–1 record. It was his worst mark as a coach, and the 211 points given up by that team were the most in school history. It clearly was time for younger ideas, and one of Crisler's disciples, Chalmers "Bump" Elliott, was waiting in the wings.

Coach Oosterbaan takes a knee with Chuck Ortmann (center) and team captain Robert Allen Wahl. Ortmann earned all-conference honors at left halfback in 1950 while Wahl was named an All-American at right tackle.

Sweet Perfection

This time there were no doubts. There was no wire service poll after the Rose Bowl, and there were no squabbles with Notre Dame partisans; a season-ending tie with Southern California took care of the Irish. A perfect 9–0 record answered all questions.

Michigan's 1948 team may not have been quite as spectacular on offense as the 1947 group that had blown out eight of its ten opponents by three touchdowns or more. The 1948 squad did that only four times. Nobody was complaining, though.

Incredibly enough, even with a 16-game winning streak Michigan entered the first AP poll of the 1948 season ranked only seventh. But after blasting Rose Bowl-bound Northwestern 28–0 in week four, the Wolverines climbed to No. 1, and that's where they finished. Because of the Big Ten's no-repeat rule for the Rose Bowl, and

Richard Kempthorn, Leo Koceski, and Chuck Ortmann (left to right) teamed in the Michigan backfield in 1948 and '49. U-M outscored its opponents 252–44 in 1948.

with no other bowl participation allowed, the great season ended with a 13–3 throttling of Ohio State in Columbus.

What made the accomplishment even more impressive was that the entire starting backfield, the celebrated Mad Magicians of 1947, was gone. In their place, coach Bennie Oosterbaan inserted a quartet of backs with only minimal experience.

Quarterback Pete Elliott didn't exactly replace his brother, Bump, who had played right halfback in 1947.

But Pete wrote his own chapter in the family archive. In his fourth season with the Wolverines, he led the way as an outstanding blocker in the single wing and even earned All-America recognition at defensive back. Pete also was Michigan's first 12-letter man, earning letters in football, basketball, and golf.

Sophomore halfbacks Chuck Ortmann and Leo Koceski provided flash and finesse, while end Dick Rifenburg won consensus All-America honors and finished second in the nation in scoring among ends.

The team drew four crowds of more than 80,000 to the Big House—the first time that had ever happened. Their toughest game, however, was a 13–7 scrap with Michigan State. That proved to be an omen of things to come.

25 Wins in a Row

The Wolverines' 25-game winning streak began on November 2, 1946, after a 13–9 loss to Illinois. It ended on October 8, 1949, with a 21–7 beating by Army. In between, they dominated.

1946				1947 cont.			1948 cont.			1949	
Minnesota	21–0			Minnesota	13–6		Northwestern	28–0			
Michigan State	55–7			Illinois	14–7		Minnesota	27–14			
Wisconsin	28–6			Indiana	35–0		Illinois	28–20			
Ohio State	58–6			Wisconsin	40–6		Navy	35–0			
				Ohio State	21–0		Indiana	54–0			
1947				USC	49–0		Ohio State	13–3			
Michigan State	55–0			1948			1949				
Stanford	49–13			Michigan State	13–7		Michigan State	7–3			
Pittsburgh	69–0			Oregon	14–0		Stanford	27–7			
Northwestern	49–21			Purdue	40–0						

The Snow Bowl

It was a game that never should have been played. One of the worst blizzards in Ohio history on the weekend after Thanksgiving, 1950, turned Columbus into Siberia. Howling winds and foot-high snowdrifts made travel and football almost impossible.

But the Buckeyes had sold some 85,000 tickets, the conference championship was riding on the outcome, and it was, after all, Michigan-Ohio State.

So in what probably was the strangest game in Michigan's history, the Wolverines prevailed 9–3 without ever making a first down. Chuck Ortmann punted 24 times, sometimes on first down, in an effort to maintain field position, which was about all that could be done.

Michigan won on two blocked punts. The first resulted in a safety, and the second was recovered by Tony Momsen in the end zone for a touchdown. No one scored in the second half. It was by then just a struggle for survival.

Linebacker Roger Zatkoff, who couldn't play because of injuries, recalled that "there were times when you could not see the field from the sidelines and none of us knew what was happening out there."

The Buckeyes were sparked by their All-American triple-threat back, Vic Janowicz, who accounted for their points with a field goal. If they had won this game, it would have clinched their second straight conference title. They were blocked from the Rose Bowl by the no-repeat rule, but beating the Wolverines and denying them the bid would have been pleasure enough.

Even with the extreme weather conditions, OSU fans climbed all over coach Wes Fesler in the postmortem. He

Besides the snow and a temperature of ten degrees, 30-mph winds howled through The Horseshoe. "My hands were numb," recalled OSU quarterback Vic Janowicz. "You knew what you wanted to do, but you couldn't do it."

was chastised for punting on third down late in the first half, which U-M turned into a touchdown. He ended up getting fired. Michigan did spend New Year's Day in sunny Pasadena. But the greatest significance of the "Snow Bowl" is that it resulted in Woody Hayes coming to Columbus.

The Sole Bowl of the '50s

No Rose Bowl should be considered an anticlimax. But after the ordeal of the "Snow Bowl," Michigan's 14–6 defeat of fifth-ranked California seemed almost mundane. This wasn't a great Michigan team. It had lost two non-conference games, had finished the regular season at 5–3–1, and had needed a season-ending upset of Ohio State to get to the bowl.

The Wolverines' play in the Rose Bowl seemed to reflect the team's lack of passion. They trailed 6–0 at the half, but after some adjustments by Ooster-baan the offense started to roll. Two fourth-quarter TDs by fullback Don Dufek—the last one with just five and a half minutes left in the game—sealed the victory. It would be Michigan's last bowl appearance for 14 years.

101,000 Plus One

The grand vision of Fielding Yost had been a stadium that seated 120,000 fans. But a rotten economy and a war intervened, and for the 21 seasons after 1927 the capacity of Michigan Stadium was stuck on 86,000, minus a few.

By 1949, however, the economy was finally thriving, and two successive unbeaten teams (1947 and '48) raised interest in Michigan football. Sellouts were occurring on a regular basis. It was time to get back to the original plan.

The "temporary" wooden bleachers that Yost had placed around the second deck in 1927 were replaced by steel stands, which expanded capacity by 11,486. The Wolverines filled the place in four of the six home games in 1949, and they led the nation in attendance—the first time that statistic was kept.

Seven years later, Michigan Stadium became the first college-owned venue to seat more than 100,000. The actual figure was 101,001—the final digit added to honor Fritz Crisler for his work in restoring the program. It reached that capacity on the second home date of the 1956 season, a 9–0 loss to Michigan State.

In this era, Michigan football began taking the form its fans love today. The team running onto the field and touching the M Club banner was introduced at the Illinois game in 1962. It must have worked. Michigan won during an otherwise drab 2–7 season. This entrance has become one of the most electrifying moments in college football.

The pregame march to the stadium by the band, and its renditions of the "Hawaiian War Chant" and "Temptation" (always played when the opposition is forced to punt),

date from these years. So does the growth of tailgate parties, Bob Ufer's frenetic descriptions of games on the radio, and planes with advertising banners circling overhead.

Unfortunately, the expansion of Michigan Stadium coincided with a decline in football success. In the first 13 years of six-figure seating, Michigan reached that figure only nine times—and eight of those were for Michigan State games when Spartan fans boosted the total.

From 1950 through 1968, Michigan's record against State was 4–13–2. The Spartans went to three Rose Bowls after entering the Big Ten in 1953, while the Wolverines went only once during that span. It was clear that gridiron dominance within the state of Michigan had turned decisively toward MSU.

Michigan super-fan Hazel Losh poses with U-M lettermen. A professor of astronomy at Michigan, Losh was a regular at football games and pep rallies for more than 50 years.

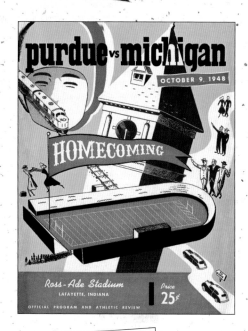

The 1948 team's national championship remains Michigan's only undisputed national football title of the last 75 years.

The Michigan defense went nearly a month without allowing a point in 1948, highlighted by a 40–0 thumping of Purdue.

After going out on top—retiring after his 10–0 season in 1947—coach Fritz Crisler unveiled his secrets in this well-received book.

Some 50,000 Ohio State fans turned out for the 1950 "Snow Bowl" despite the worst blizzard in Columbus in 37 years.

Michigan players practice covertly—or so they hope—in September 1949. U-M extended its winning streak to 25 games on October 1 before falling to Army.

Bulldozing fullback Don Dufek, Sr., was Michigan's MVP in 1950. As illustrator Frank Williams suggests, teams practically needed to build a brick wall to stop him.

Down 6–0 at the half in the 1951 Rose Bowl, U-M outgained Cal 226–52 in the last two quarters en route to a 14–6 victory.

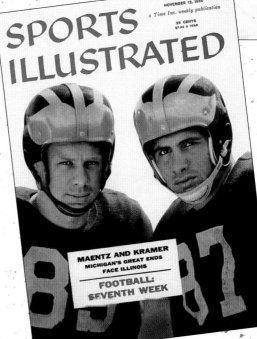

Right end Tom Maentz (left) captained the 1956 Wolverines while left end Ron Kramer was the team's MVP—for the third year in a row.

Stars of the '50s and '60s

First came Tom Harmon on the cover of *Life* in 1940. Then it was Bob Chappuis on *Time* in 1947. Ron Kramer and Tom Maentz kept Michigan's connection with the Luce magazine empire alive when they appeared on the cover of *Sports Illustrated* in 1956. They were billed as "Michigan's great ends."

Kramer and Maentz led the Wolverines to two straight 7–2 seasons in the mid-'50s, the team's best records between the conference championships of 1950 and 1964. The 1956 team wound up ranked No. 7 in the country, but neither one of these squads won the Big Ten title. Both losses each year came within the conference, and that was enough to eliminate them.

Kramer was recognized as the greatest end to play for Michigan since Bennie Oosterbaan. "Nothing was impossible for him," said Oosterbaan of Kramer, whom he coached. "The impossible was only a challenge."

Kramer frequently played both ways during his career, and he was as prized for his fierce defense and smash-mouth blocking ability as for his pass-catching. In basketball, he set a school scoring mark that lasted into the 1960s. Remarkably for a man of his 230-pound stature, he was also an adept high jumper, lettering in track for three years. When Kramer turned pro, Vince Lombardi redefined the position of tight end at Green Bay to fit the receiver's special talents.

Ron Kramer excelled as a receiver, defensive end, and kicker—and sometimes filled in at running back. He also captained the basketball team and excelled in the high jump.

Though he is remembered by few, Jack Clancy was a prolific pass receiver. In 1966 he became the first Michigan player to top 1,000 receiving yards in one season—and one of only two Wolverines to do so in the 20th century.

Jim Pace, billed as "the fastest ever at Michigan" when he arrived in Ann Arbor, starred at halfback on those teams and led the conference in rushing in 1957. He was paired with Terry Barr, an outstanding receiver and kick returner, who went on to a long career with the Detroit Lions.

A big part of Michigan's problem in this era was that it held itself above the sordid recruiting process. While Michigan State and Duffy Daugherty were going after outstanding African American athletes from the segregated South, Michigan relied on its reputation to attract talent. It didn't work out too well.

One exception was Bill Yearby, one of the fastest tackles in the country and deadly on pursuit as a defender. Alumni finally persuaded the coaching staff to target him when he played high school ball in Detroit, and Yearby anchored an outstanding defense in 1964 when Michigan finally broke through with a conference title.

A few years later, the Wolverines went into Detroit again and came away with Ron Johnson, one of the most punishing runners ever to play at Michigan. He broke almost every rushing record in school history. In his final home game, in 1968, he ran for 347 yards in a 34–9 pummeling of Wisconsin. That established an NCAA record. Johnson scored five touchdowns in the game, and he finished the season with a conference-record 92 points against Big Ten competition. Unfortunately, his career coincided with that of O. J. Simpson, and he never won the national recognition he deserved. It also didn't help that Michigan never played in a bowl game during his stay.

Through the mid- and late '60s, the flow of talent deepened, although it added up to only one Big Ten championship for coach Bump Elliott, in 1964. Split end Jack Clancy, a converted quarterback, broke all Michigan receiving records in 1966 and accounted for two thirds of the team's total receiving yardage. He went on to star with the Miami Dolphins.

Another erstwhile quarterback was Rick Volk, who stopped throwing passes in order to intercept them. He became a star at safety on the 1966 team. A nephew of Chappuis, he also started games at fullback in that same season, making him one of the most versatile performers in school history. He went on to a great pro career with the Baltimore Colts.

Michigan slowly converted from the single wing to the wing T formation, although its offense was among the last in the country to retain some plays from the older formation. In 1964 Bob Timberlake became the team's first great passer from the T. At 6'4", he was the prototype of the bigger quarterbacks that would soon become the standard with this offensive set. He also kicked field goals and extra points, and his total offense of 1,381 yards in '64 (excluding the bowl game) ranked second in school history.

Coach Bump Elliott felt comfortable with quarterback Bob Timberlake at the controls. The three-year starter earned Academic All-Big Ten honors in 1963 and '64.

Bump in the Road

If ever a man seemed to be the perfect choice to coach Michigan, it was Bump Elliott. He had been a leader of the 1947 national champions, and in Fritz Crisler's words, he was "the best right halfback I ever saw."

Elliott understudied at Iowa under another man steeped in the Michigan tradition, Forest Evashevski. Bump became the Wolverines' head coach at age 34, making him the youngest coach in the Big Ten. Bright and affable, Elliott brought in the wing T, opening up the offense after a decade of stodgy Michigan football.

The only problem was that he didn't win—or rather, he didn't win enough. Elliott took Michigan to its only Rose Bowl over an 18-year span in 1964. But of the 11 losing seasons Michigan endured in the 20th century, five came on his ten-year watch.

Most of all, Elliott could not beat Woody Hayes. He was 3–7 against Ohio State, and on two nightmarish occasions the Buckeyes rang up 50 points on Elliott's squads. To make it worse, they were two of his better teams.

When Michigan finally decided it had to be proactive in recruiting top players, Elliott was masterful at it. A steady stream of major talent began flowing into Ann Arbor beginning in the mid-1960s. These guys loved playing for him, too. When Elliott became the first man ever to play for and coach Michigan in the Rose Bowl, he endeared himself to the U-M faithful—at least for a while.

When he had taken over for Bennie Oosterbaan in 1959, Bump had promised a conference championship in five years. It took six. He actually had the team ranked as high as sixth in the country in his third season, but that

Bump Elliott in 1959 opens his first fall practice as Wolverines head coach. Despite serving with the Marines during World War II, Elliott was criticized for being too soft on his players.

season ended with a thud when OSU took the Wolverines apart at Michigan Stadium 50–20.

Then in 1968 the Wolverines ran off an eight-game winning streak, their longest in 20 years, and they went into Columbus ranked fourth in the nation. Woody's national champions destroyed that team 50–14, and although the OSU players always denied that it was meant as a final sneer, the Buckeyes went for a two-point conversion after the final TD.

Even after an 8–2 season, Elliott could not survive that kind of humiliation. Throughout the 1960s, many had wondered whether Elliott, unlike Woody, had been too easy on his players. After the 1968 season, the Michigan brass decided that they needed a different type of coach. They needed Bo Schembechler.

A Foot Short of Perfection

Maybe the best thing about the 1964 title run was its total surprise. Michigan had just come off two straight losing seasons, winning a grand total of five games. There didn't seem to be much basis for optimism. True, the defense had shown a vast improvement in the middle of the previous season, and Michigan had even upset conference champion Illinois at Champaign. But it still had added up to a fifth-place finish.

However, in the third week of 1964, the Wolverines went up to East Lansing and knocked off ninth-ranked MSU 17–10 with two fourth-quarter scores. It was clear that this was a different kind of Bump Elliott team.

In fact, Michigan would miss running the board by the margin of one agonizing foot and one slender point. That's how close Bob Timberlake came to the end zone when he was tackled on a two-point conversion try in a 21–20 loss to Purdue. Timberlake had just run 54 yards for a touch-

Beavers Are Believers

As the 1964 season concluded, Southern California was the popular choice to be Michigan's Rose Bowl opponent. The Trojans had ruined Notre Dame's unbeaten season on the final Saturday, and in the Pac-8 they had suffered just a one-point loss to Washington. But Oregon State tied USC in the standings, and the teams did not meet. Under conference rules, in the case of a tie the most recent Rose Bowl team was out, meaning the Beavers were in.

Oregon State was no match for the Wolverines. Long runs by Mel Anthony (84 yards) and Carl Ward sent Michigan to a 12–7 halftime lead. Then they poured it on, with Anthony scoring twice more in the third quarter. Michigan rolled up 332 yards on the ground in an overwhelming 34–7 win. The Wolverines were now a perfect 4–0 in the Rose Bowl.

Michigan quarterback Bob Timberlake rambles for nine yards against Oregon State in the Rose Bowl. Just one yard would have given him a two-point conversion and a win over Purdue, the only team to defeat Michigan in 1964.

down to set up the conversion try. The upset that ruined the perfect season was engineered by sophomore quarterback Bob Griese. It was his son, Brian, who would lead Michigan to their next perfect campaign, 33 years later.

A tie in the standings favored Purdue, and for most of the year it seemed that Michigan would be deprived of a Pasadena trip by that single point. But the Boilermakers lost twice in the last three weeks. Now all that stood between Michigan and the Rose Bowl was Ohio State. Unbeaten in the Big Ten and ranked No. 7 in the country, the Buckeyes hosted Michigan at Columbus, where the Wolverines hadn't won since 1936.

Overcoming the odds, Michigan prevailed. The defense shut down the Buckeyes completely, and Timberlake's field goal and TD pass to Jim Detwiler were all the Wolverines needed in a 10–0 win. That defense, anchored by tackle Bill Yearby, allowed just 76 points during the regular season, the best mark since the undefeated bunch of 1948.

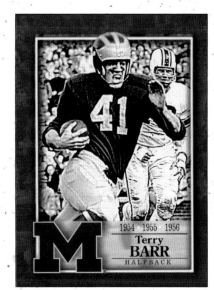

Halfback Terry Barr, Michigan's MVP in 1955, went on to an All-Pro career as a wide receiver with the Detroit Lions.

The Michigan Daily

HOW THE WEST WIS WON:

Wolverines Cop Roses, Clobber Beavers, 34-7

Long Runs Spark Offense: Anthony Ties Bowl Record

'M' Gridders Post Perfect Record In Four Rose Bowl Appearances

By BILL BULLARD

...agers Upset Twice; ...halk Up Four Wins

VOTED MVP: *Anthony: Nobody Touched Me*

An 11-point favorite in the 1965 Rose Bowl, Michigan won by much more. Mel Anthony ran for three touchdowns, including an 84-yard burst.

Henry Hatch, Michigan's equipment manager for decades, ties a ribbon around the Little Brown Jug, the second oldest trophy in college football.

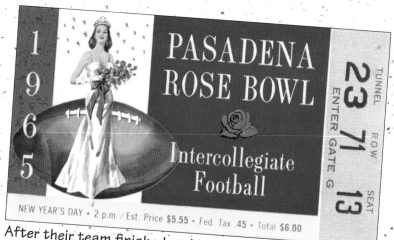

1965 PASADENA ROSE BOWL Intercollegiate Football

NEW YEAR'S DAY • 2 p.m. / Est. Price $5.55 • Fed. Tax .45 • Total $6.00

TUNNEL 23 ROW 71 SEAT 13 ENTER GATE G

After their team finished no higher than fifth in the Big Ten for seven straight years, Wolverines fans cherished their tickets to the 1965 Rose Bowl.

A vendor hawks pennants, flowers, and assorted trinkets outside Michigan Stadium on a pleasant football Saturday.

MICHIGAN STATE Spartans
MICHIGAN Wolverines

SPARTAN GRIDIRON NEWS 50¢   Souvenir Program   October 8, 1966 SPARTAN STADIUM Kickoff 1:30 p.m.

The Spartans did indeed bag the Wolverines in 1966, winning 20–7 during their last undefeated season of the 20th century.

MICHIGAN   OHIO STATE

NOVEMBER 23, 1968 · OFFICIAL PROGRAM · FIFTY CENTS

Buckeye nuts fell on the Wolverines in 1968, as Ohio State humiliated Michigan 50–14. U-M would get revenge 12 months later.

This Michigan fan puppet could do the "Hail! Hail!" fist pump during the singing of "The Victors."

Classic Games

The 21 seasons in which Bennie Oosterbaan and Bump Elliott coached Michigan have largely fallen down the memory hole. They are recalled as the long intermission between the brilliant regimes of Fritz Crisler and Bo Schembechler, an era in which losing seasons arose with disturbing frequency.

A few games do stand out: the Rose Bowl wins following the 1950 and 1964 campaigns; the 1950 Snow Bowl at Ohio State; and the 10–0 shutout at Columbus in 1964. However, only a few other games from that era are fondly recalled. Several of them occurred during the 1955 and 1956 seasons, two almost-great years that might have been.

On October 8, 1955, Michigan demolished Army 26–2 before a record crowd of 97,366. It was Michigan's first victory ever over the Cadets, who had beaten the Wolverines five times. That win launched U-M to No. 1 in the AP poll for the first time since 1949. However, November losses to Illinois and Ohio State doomed their season.

In 1956 Michigan beat Iowa 17–14 in a thriller that was decided by a touchdown with 66 seconds left in the game. It was the only loss Iowa suffered all season. But Michigan had been undone the previous week when Minnesota's Bobby Cox, leading a hurry-up attack that could run off four plays in a minute, befuddled the defense in a 20–7 defeat. Coupled with an earlier loss to Michigan State, it cost the Wolverines a visit to Pasadena.

> "In one of the most shocking routs of this or any other season, Bennie Oosterbaan's Wolverines manhandled the West Point cadets in a 26–2 triumph."
>
> *The New York Times,* October 9, 1955

When Michigan beat Woody Hayes's first OSU team, 7–0 in 1951, the coach reportedly was so furious while viewing the game films with his staff that he picked up the projector and threw it across the room. A much sadder meeting took place in 1963. The traditional season finale was delayed for a week after the assassination of President John F. Kennedy. There were no bowl implications, and when it was played in Ann Arbor only 36,424 people showed up to watch the Buckeyes win 14–10. A grieving nation had other things on its mind. Earlier in 1963, Michigan handed Illinois (led by legendary linebacker Dick Butkus) its only loss of the season, a stunning 14–8 upset in Champaign. The Illini were then ranked No. 2 in the nation.

Maybe the oddest run of games came during an otherwise ordinary 1967 season, in which Michigan finished 4–6. No fewer than six games were decided in the last ten minutes. Unfortunately, Michigan lost four of them—to California, Navy, Indiana, and Minnesota—within a five-week span. Local merchants call such contests "trunk-slammers," because all their customers want to do afterward is return to their cars and go home.

This was also when Hayes built up his portfolio against Michigan. After the initial blanking in 1951, he went 12–5. The most maddening for Michigan came in 1965, when neither team was in the running for anything. After leading 7–6 for most of the game, Michigan lost when Ohio State's Bob Funk nailed a 28-yard field goal with 75 ticks left. It was the closest game between the teams in 16 years, and a harbinger of duels to come.

Michigan guard Charles Krahnke (62) clears the way for halfback Tony Branoff during Michigan's stunning 26–2 triumph over Army in 1955.

Green and Blue

Paul Bunyan was the mythical lumberjack who roamed the north woods. Since 1953, Paul also has stood—hands on hips, ax at his feet—on the trophy awarded to the winner of the Michigan-Michigan State game.

Michigan was not exactly thrilled when Governor G. Mennen Williams (a Princeton man) announced that the trophy would be awarded after MSU joined the Big Ten in 1953. The Wolverines loved tradition, and they already were playing Minnesota for the Little Brown Jug. Wasn't that enough? Besides, those troublesome people down in Columbus seemed to be under the impression that their game with Michigan was the biggest of the season. On top of all that, State was hot.

Under former Michigan assistant Biggie Munn, the Spartans had turned into a powerhouse—national champions, in fact, in 1952. Until the 1950 season, Michigan's record against State had been 33–6–3, but now the Spartans were spitting fire. So Fritz Crisler told the governor thanks, but no thanks. Michigan was not interested in accepting such a trophy.

He need not have worried. The Rose Bowl-bound Spartans beat Michigan for the fourth straight time in 1953, 14–6. But when the Wolverines finally broke through in 1954 with a thorough 33–7 clocking of State, they were only too happy to grab Big Paul.

But that was something of an aberration. Under Munn and Duffy Daugherty, State simply dominated Michigan throughout the 1950s and '60s. In the first 16 years after the inception of the trophy, Michigan's record in the series

The Paul Bunyan Trophy is awarded annually to the winner of the Michigan State-Michigan game. Some scholars claim that the mythical Bunyan was based on a Michigan lumberjack named Fabian "Saginaw Joe" Fournier.

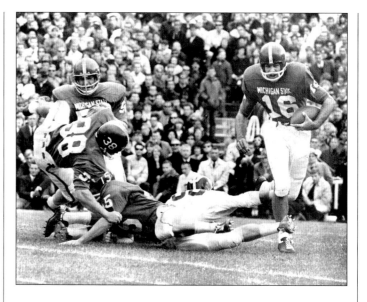

Prior to their 1964 matchup (pictured), Michigan State had gone 6–0–2 against their hated rival over the previous eight years. But the Wolverines prevailed in this classic contest 17–10.

was 4–10–2. These weren't nail-biters, either. MSU shut out the Wolverines four times—including 28–0 drubbings in 1961 and 1962—and outscored them by an overall margin of 307–162.

In the nasty words of a *Michigan Daily* writer of the era, "I'm so sick of losing to State that I can't look a cow in the face anymore." That was cold. But the game was never played before less than a capacity crowd, at Ann Arbor or East Lansing, for every year during this period.

Michigan did play the great 1966 State team tough before going down 20–7 in East Lansing. It gave the unbeaten Spartans one of their closest contests before MSU's classic 10–10 finale with Notre Dame. But this was a period in which State out-recruited Michigan in state and out, dominated media coverage, and made Paul Bunyan their personal possession.

Just Shy of Great in '68

The Bump Elliott regime finally seemed to have reached its pinnacle by 1968. Aggressive recruiting had brought in the deepest pool of talent that Michigan had seen in more than a decade.

Senior quarterback Dennis Brown ran an offense that racked up 277 points in '68, the most since the fabled Mad Magicians of 21 years before. Brown fired passes to end Jim Mandich. Ron Johnson was an electrifying runner, and an offensive line led by Dan Dierdorf opened gaping holes for him. The defense featured future U-M athletic director Tom Goss at tackle, Tom Curtis at safety, and Henry Hill at middle guard.

With 1,391 yards rushing in 1968, Ron Johnson (left) established the Michigan single-season record. His 347 rushing yards against Wisconsin that year broke the NCAA single-game record.

After a sputtering 21–7 loss to California, this group started to roll. Only Indiana, the defending Big Ten champs, came close to them, going down 27–22 at Bloomington. In the three games before meeting Ohio State, Michigan outscored its foes 105–9 and rose to No. 4 in the national poll.

But Woody Hayes had put together, in his opinion, "prob-ably the best team that ever played college football." OSU featured All-Americans on both sides of the ball—tackle Dave Foley and fullback Jim Otis on offense, and guard Jim Stillwagon and cornerback Jack Tatum on defense.

On paper, Michigan appeared to be their match, with maybe even a bit of an edge on defense. Unfortunately, Michigan had one big flaw: It did not really believe it could beat undefeated OSU. Hayes held a 6–3 lead over Elliott, including the 50–20 mauling in 1961, and the memory stayed.

The Buckeyes broke it open in the second half, scoring 29 points. Michigan could not contain the deception of quarterback Rex Kern and the relentless pounding of Otis, who scored four touchdowns. It was the final TD of the 50–14 drubbing, and the ensuing two-point conversion try, that both infuriated Michigan fans and led to Elliott's resignation as coach.

Did Hayes Run Up the Score?

With the score 50–14 and 1:24 remaining, did Woody Hayes really call for the two-point conversion? Michigan adherents swore he did, and they swore revenge. Some of the coaches even shouted curses at Hayes as they left the field. Hayes fueled the fire when asked why he did it by responding, "Because I couldn't go for three."

But others on the Ohio State team denied that was Woody's intent. According to Jim Otis, the last TD was scored by reserves, and there was such excitement that they forgot to get the kicking team on the field. They felt that calling a timeout at that point would have been an even greater slight to Michigan. So Otis called for a two-point play instead, which failed. At least, that's the Buckeye version.

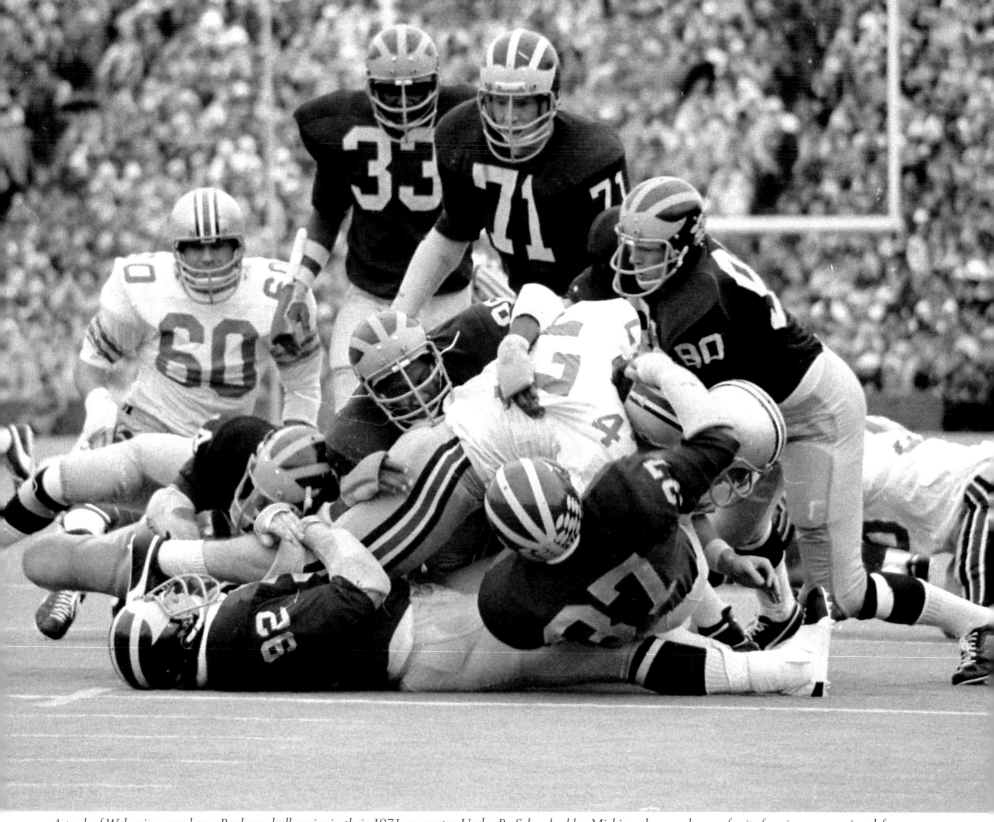

A pack of Wolverines crushes a Buckeyes ballcarrier in their 1971 encounter. Under Bo Schembechler, Michigan became known for its ferocious, swarming defense.

Bo's Boys

1969–1989

Michigan football is reborn under Bo Schembechler. His 21-year regime is highlighted by ten brilliant battles against Woody Hayes, dominance of the Big Ten, repeated bowl trips, no losing seasons, an endless succession of All-Americans, and renewed pride in the maize and blue.

Right: Coach Bo Schembechler felt confident about his 1970 team, a club that won its first nine games before losing to Ohio State. Above: Bo never enjoyed a perfect season, but he would have if the Wolverines had beaten Stanford in the 1972 Rose Bowl. They lost by a single point.

Meet Mr. Schembechler

For the first time in 31 years, Michigan was going outside the program to choose a coach, and it was about as far outside as it could get. They picked someone who came from the maw of the enemy—a student of Woody Hayes and Ohio State football.

Bo Schembechler had played for Hayes as an undersized lineman at Miami of Ohio, and then became his top assistant in Columbus. They were the closest of antagonists even then, and when Bo got the chance to leave and head the program at Miami, he jumped at it.

> ## "I didn't like that SOB when he played for me, I didn't like him when he worked for me, and I certainly don't like him now."
>
> ### Woody Hayes on Bo Schembechler

This was the man Michigan picked after a nationwide search in the autumn of 1968. He had been the darkest of dark horses for the job. Almost no one had heard of him in Ann Arbor. He checked into a local hotel the night before his introduction under the name of Glenn Schem. That was an unnecessary precaution. If he had used his own name, he never would have been recognized.

Schembechler understood two things instinctively. The first was that his new team was soft. It lacked both the physical and mental toughness to beat the best. That would have to change—and pretty damn quickly, too.

The second thing was the force of Michigan's football tradition. It may have gone through some fallow years, but it was still the team of Yost and Crisler, Harmon and Oosterbaan, Chappuis and Kramer. When one of his assistants complained about the dinginess of their dressing area, Bo told him that Fielding Yost may have hung his clothes on the same wall hook. He would use that tradition as the beacon to light the path to where Michigan football had to return. He would accept nothing less.

Returning players were stunned at the regimen he installed. He headed ferocious practices, the likes of which none of them had ever experienced. The walk-ons quit in droves. Bo put up a sign: "Those who stay will be champions." He wasn't a man who made rash promises, either.

Over time, the Michigan players noticed something. They always seemed better prepared than their opponents. In the fourth quarter when the other team started to sag, they were still going full tilt. They may have hated Bo, but during games their fury was concentrated and direct.

He did make one error, though. From day one in Ann Arbor, his focus was on beating Ohio State. Nothing else mattered. Not the loss to Missouri in week three of the

Schembechler's offensive philosophy was simple: Wear down opposing defenses with the running game until they were pudding by the fourth quarter.

1969 season and not the loss to Michigan State in week five. But it turned out that the MSU game *did* matter, and after the 23–12 pasting the media was full of descriptions of how old Duffy Daugherty had handled the new kid. Bo never lost to him again.

Schembechler gave intensity a headache. He carried a yardstick with him during practices and swatted players with it when they goofed up. He swore that a Michigan team might lose but it would never be outhit. Most of all, he insisted on a program that was clean beyond question. Nothing under the table or even at the edge of the rules was tolerated.

And in the end, the players who cursed under their breath at him as redshirts and sophomores left Michigan

Bo became a little less gruff late in his career, but he never lost the respect of his players.

Woody Hayes (right) on Schembechler: "We respected one another so damn much. Now that doesn't mean I didn't get so mad at him that I wanted to kick him in the, uh, groin."

loving the man. They knew that whatever happened later in life, Bo would be there for them.

Schembechler had walked onto one of the most radically politicized campuses of the '60s, and through the force of his personality and methods restored the virtues of discipline and hard work. Of course, if Michigan hadn't won, it would have all been a joke.

But the Wolverines did win. In each of Bo's first ten seasons, he finished ranked among the nation's top ten. In his 21 seasons, he captured 13 conference championships and went to ten Rose Bowls. He built a program so strong that it forced the Big Ten to change its rules regarding bowl eligibility.

In 1969, however, that was still in the future. Bo won the biggest game of his life that November, and he almost lost his life one month later. There was much, much more to come.

An Upset for the Ages

A 60-yard punt return by Barry Pierson (pictured) put Michigan at the 3 in the middle of the second quarter. The subsequent touchdown and extra point gave the Wolverines a comfortable 21–12 lead.

Rarely has the world of college football changed as quickly and emphatically as it did on November 22, 1969. A frenzied group of Wolverines pulled one of the greatest upsets in the long history of Michigan football, beating Ohio State 24–12 and immediately restoring the program to the upper rank of the sport.

Even those who were part of the record crowd of 103,588 at Michigan Stadium didn't quite believe what they were seeing. The 1969 Buckeyes already had been anointed the greatest team of the '60s. They were averaging 46 points a game entering the Michigan contest, and had absolutely destroyed every team they had played. Michigan's spot in the Rose Bowl was clinched because of the conference's no-repeat rule, but it had lost twice. The Wolverines were 17-point underdogs. No one seriously

Whoever bought this ticket likely considered it the best $6 he or she ever spent. The atmosphere throughout the game was electric. In the waning moments fans sang, "Goodbye, Woody, goodbye!"

expected them to handle OSU, the team that had humiliated them just one year before.

No one believed it except their new head coach, Glenn "Bo" Schembechler, and the players he had turned into believers. From the day he arrived in Ann Arbor 11 months earlier, he had dedicated himself to preparing for this game and building up his team's discipline and confidence.

That's what had been lacking from the talent-laden squad assembled by his predecessor, Bump Elliott. When the Wolverines took the field that afternoon, they were absolutely convinced that they were a match for Woody Hayes's Buckeyes.

Although the crowd was record-sized and the first home sellout against OSU since 1957, it was not wholly partisan. Athletic director Don Canham had released many thousands of seats to Buckeye supporters on the expectation that they would not be sold to Michigan fans. He would never have to do anything like that again.

The game itself has passed into legend. Ohio State scored easily on its second series of downs, as Jim Otis scored his fifth TD against Michigan in the last two years. But then quarterback Don Moorhead answered, bring-

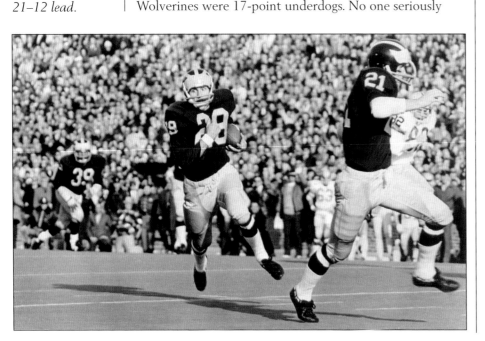

ing the Wolverines right down the field by mixing passes to Jim Mandich with runs up the gut by fullback Garvie Craw. Michigan moved ahead 7–6, and the unexpected drive inspired the massive crowd.

But Ohio State was unshaken. Aided by a pass interference penalty, Rex Kern moved OSU downfield and then hit Jan White on a 22-yard touchdown pass. The Buckeyes were back in front, 12–7. No one could have guessed it, but they were done for the day. From there on, it was all Michigan.

On the next possession, Moorhead carved up the Buckeye defense. After halfback Billy Taylor broke loose on a 28-yard run, Craw barreled into the end zone for a second time. Michigan led 14–12 and then forced Ohio State to punt the ball, which Michigan defensive back

Bo Suffers a Heart Attack

The feel-good story had a downer of an ending. On the night before the Rose Bowl, Bo Schembechler began experiencing tightness in his chest. He was taken to the hospital as a precaution, and he was told that he had suffered a heart attack.

The team didn't know that any of this had happened until an announcement was made right before the players took the field. Completely stunned, they could not get organized on offense against a good, fifth-ranked Southern California team. The attack that had averaged 35 points a game was held to a field goal, and the final was 10–3. Bo recovered nicely, but the medical condition would shadow the rest of his career.

The odds-makers who made Ohio State a 17-point favorite underestimated the will of the Wolverines. Said Bo, "We knew we were going to win from the very beginning."

Barry Pierson returned 60 yards to the 3. Moorhead took it in himself, giving Michigan a 21–12 cushion. After another touchdown was nullified by a penalty, the Wolverines kicked a field goal to give them a 24–12 lead at the half.

The stadium braced for a big Buckeye comeback, but OSU could get nothing going. Players said later that it was as if Bo was in their huddle and in Woody's head, anticipating everything that his mentor was going to call.

Kern could not cope with the suffocating Michigan run defense. Safety Tom Curtis intercepted two of his passes, and by the fourth quarter Kern was so utterly frustrated that he had to be replaced. The Buckeyes not only were beaten, they were beaten thoroughly.

The second half was scoreless, and the game ended 24–12. The players carried off Bo on their shoulders, while students tore down the goalposts. The next stop was Pasadena. "We're going as co-champions of the Big Ten," Bo declared, "and don't you forget it!"

The Michigan Juggernaut

Despite the exultation about the big win over OSU in 1969 ("Goody, Goody. Bo Beat Woody," read the bumper stickers), the renewed enthusiasm was slow to translate at the box office. In 1970 the only sellout, as usual, was for Michigan State. The average attendance for the other five home games was only 74,517, and it was about the same in 1971, with the exception of a capacity crowd for Ohio State.

But the performance on the field had changed enormously. The momentum established in 1969 was now a tidal wave. The 1970 Wolverines rolled over everyone, with only Texas A&M giving U-M a challenge. Michigan needed a touchdown with three minutes to play to pull out that 14–10 win.

However, Woody Hayes was waiting in Columbus. He got a piece of revenge with a 20–9 win, ruining Michigan's perfect season and sending the Bucks back to Pasadena. It was obvious that from now on these Michigan-Ohio State games were going to be more intense and bruising than anything previously known in the long history of the series.

In 1971 Bo pushed the Wolverines at an even higher level. Their total of 409 points in the 11-game regular season was the best since the Point-a-Minute teams of the early 1900s. On successive weeks, they shattered Indiana 61–7 and Iowa 63–7. Then they finished off a perfect conference season on Billy Taylor's bolt into the end zone with 2:07 to go in a 10–7 win over OSU before another record home crowd.

In the Rose Bowl, a crushing 13–12 loss to Stanford on a field goal with 16 seconds left took away a little luster.

Halfback Billy Taylor barrels through the Stanford defense for a touchdown in the 1972 Rose Bowl. Had the Cardinal missed its last-minute field goal, Michigan would have had its first undefeated season since 1948.

Contrary to legend, though, it didn't cost Michigan a national championship. Despite the unbeaten season, the Wolverines were ranked only fourth entering the game, and the title went to undefeated Nebraska.

The Mellow Men

They styled themselves the "Mellow Men of Michigan," and their house off campus was named the Den of the Mellow Men. This group of African American players, all of whom were recruited at about the same time, became the new face of football at Michigan.

The program had been slow to compete for outstanding black athletes, which was one big reason why Michigan had lagged behind Michigan State in the 1950s and '60s. Led by tailback Billy Taylor, wingback Glenn Doughty, All-American lineman Reggie McKenzie, and defensive back Thom Darden, the Mellow Men were serene only off the field. McKenzie, for one, loved to lay a hard hit on an opponent. As he put it, "It's like . . . when you bite into a piece of apple pie and say, 'Ohhhh, that's good.'"

Mellow, yes, but ferocious.

The Voice of the Wolverines

He began his broadcasting career with a tiny Ann Arbor station in 1945. Upon his death 36 years later, Bob Ufer had become the voice of Michigan football, and his play-by-play was carried by the network's flagship station, WJR in Detroit.

Ufer's heartfelt, passionate descriptions of the games became almost as much fun as watching them in person in the Big House. In the 1970s, when the allure of the Wolverines' success on the field began attracting legions of new fans, Ufer also reached new heights of popularity. He had been a track star at Michigan, and his primary business was running a successful insurance agency. But on autumn Saturdays, he seemed to adopt another persona. Ufer was as much a part of the Michigan football scene as the Block M formation.

His cry of "Touchdown, Billy Taylor! Touchdown, Billy Taylor!" when the winning TD against Ohio State was scored in 1971 became a classic. So was his description of Anthony Carter's game-ending race for the end zone against Indiana in 1979. Bob had audacious nicknames for the stars (such as Butch "Don't Call Me Harold" Woolfolk), and his Ufer-isms were hilarious. A player ran downfield "like a bunny with its tail on fire" or like "a penguin with a hot herring in his cummerbund."

Someone sent Ufer a horn that allegedly came from the staff car of George Patton during World War II, and during moments of exultation he tooted it repeatedly while comparing Bo's leadership to that other general. Less known was the counseling he gave Michigan players. He advised them to keep a positive attitude and prepare for their lives after football.

"So many announcers these days sound as if they're reading off a stat sheet," said Keith Mitchell, a former Michigan player turned Hollywood screenwriter. "Ufer's broadcasts came from the heart."

His mournful wail of "no good . . . no good" when a last-ditch field goal attempt sailed wide against Purdue in 1976 and ruined an unbeaten season carried in it the bleak despair of Michigan fans everywhere. He was still at the microphone until ten days before his death from cancer in 1981, calling the Iowa game. Unfortunately, it was a Michigan loss.

It is much better to remember Bob Ufer for his triumphant bellow in an earlier Michigan win. "Big Ed Shuttlesworth is electrocuting this crowd!" he exclaimed.

> "This crowd at Ohio Stadium is made up of 10,000 alumni and 74,000 truck drivers."
>
> **Bob Ufer**

Ufer was as big of a Michigan "fan" as coach Bo Schembechler. Both were born on April Fools' Day.

The Michigan Daily

WE'RE NUMBER ONE!!
'M' BLASTS BUCKS, 24-12

Wolverines bust Woody

Blue goes to coast

163,588 go wild after Wolverine victory

Michigan Stadium was bedlam throughout U-M's upset of Ohio State in 1969. After the game, fans stormed the field and tore down the goalposts.

MICHIGAN vs INDIANA
Michigan Stadium Ann Arbor, Michigan October 25, 1975 $1

Entering the 1975 season, Bo Schembechler's record stood at 58–7–1, giving him a better winning percentage than Yost and Crisler.

Michigan players celebrate after their exhilarating victory over Ohio State in 1969. In the opposing locker room, Woody Hayes made a brief statement and then closed the room to reporters.

Under coaches Bo Schembechler and Gary Moeller, Michigan players were awarded for particular achievements with helmet stickers (pictured).

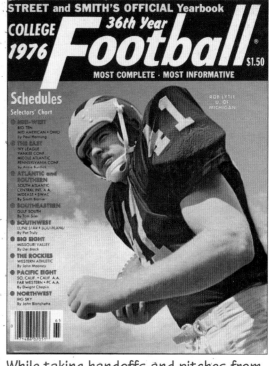

While taking handoffs and pitches from Rick Leach in 1976, Rob Lytle rushed for a school record-breaking 1,469 yards (6.65 yards per carry).

Bo Schembechler and star offensive tackle Dan Dierdorf examine how the team's cleats grip the Tartan Turf. During his All-Pro NFL career, and later as a broadcaster, Dierdorf often griped about playing for the coach he loved.

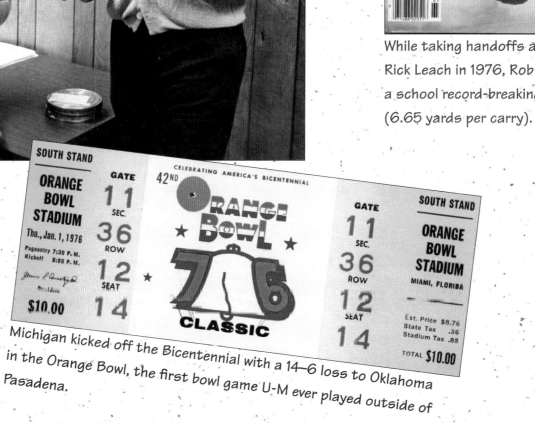

Michigan kicked off the Bicentennial with a 14–6 loss to Oklahoma in the Orange Bowl, the first bowl game U-M ever played outside of Pasadena.

The Ten-Year War

Military terminology is greatly overworked as a metaphor in football. And yet in describing the ten classic games in which Bo Schembechler and Woody Hayes collided, there probably is no better word than *war*. From 1969 through 1978, at least one of the two teams was ranked sixth or higher in the national polls. Three times a No. 1 ranking was at stake. On every occasion, the Big Ten championship and a trip to the Rose Bowl was on the line.

A series that had always been one of the best in college football was now elevated to the greatest rivalry in all of sports. The two coaches, mirror images of each other, threw everything they had into these meetings, and their teams played with an intensity that can only be described as combative. Anyone who saw one of these games came away with the certain knowledge that they had just witnessed the best that college football had to offer.

OSU players yank down the M Club banner prior to the 1973 game in Ann Arbor. "Oh, they'll meet a dastardly fate for that!" exclaimed Michigan broadcaster Bob Ufer. Fans sat through a cold drizzle only to see the game end in a 10–10 tie.

Michigan quarterback Rick Leach signals a touchdown as Roosevelt Smith (26) submarines into the end zone in the 1977 Ohio State game. Michigan won 14–6—the eighth game of the year in which it held its opponent to under ten points.

The final tally was five for Bo, four for Woody, and one infamous tie. During one game, an infuriated Hayes started throwing the yard markers around the turf in a fury. In another, the Ohio State players went after the M Club banner as they entered the field at the Big House.

Indeed, this was as close as football could come to war. And while penalties were rare, the emotions of two great midwestern states (well, maybe not the Spartan part of Michigan) rode on the outcome.

Woody loathed the very name Michigan. He insisted on referring to it as "that school up north." On those rare occasions when he felt compelled to recruit a player from Michigan, he refused to spend a dime in the state. He understood from the beginning that coaches in Columbus rose and fell on their success against Michigan.

What heightened these meetings was that Bo had been Woody's star pupil, his trusted assistant at Ohio State. Hayes planned for Schembechler to succeed him, but Bo

Michigan players carry Bo Schembechler off the field after their 1978 victory over Ohio State. The Buckeyes had to settle for the Gator Bowl, where Woody Hayes punched a Clemson player —the incident that caused him to be fired.

No other Big Ten team went to the Rose Bowl during this span. Not until 1981, in fact, was the duopoly broken (by Illinois).

When Hayes was forced out after the 1978 season for striking an opposing player in a bowl game, the series lost most of its punch. The rivalry would remain spirited, and the game would usually mean a lot. But the decade of total war was over.

knew that he could grow old before Woody finally decided to step down. So when he ended up at Michigan, of all places, and then upset Woody's greatest team the first time out of the box, the fever went off the charts.

The two men also admired each other enormously. Hayes said that, despite the stories, they had never thrown chairs at each other when Schembechler was his assistant. For his part, Bo came away with a lifelong admiration for Woody's uncompromising work ethic and the passion that went into his preparation.

In five of these games, the difference between them was a touchdown or less, and from 1971 through '74 it was never more than three points. Twice the outcome hung on field goal tries in the final minute. Bo was severely criticized for stubbornly passing up an almost certain field goal that would have tied the 1972 game. He insisted on scoring a touchdown, but failed.

The Battles

1969 Michigan 24, OSU 12: The upset sets the new tone for this series and changes everything in Ann Arbor.

1970 OSU 20, Michigan 9: Woody gets his revenge and finishes the regular season undefeated.

1971 Michigan 10, OSU 7: Billy Taylor scores the winner and Hayes rips up the sideline markers. Michigan goes to the Rose Bowl.

1972 OSU 14, Michigan 11. Two Buckeye goal-line stands decide the game.

1973 Michigan 10, OSU 10: Both finish undefeated, but the Big Ten votes to send Ohio State to the Rose Bowl for the second straight year.

1974 OSU 12, Michigan 10: Mike Lantry's game-winning field goal attempt sails wide in the last minute.

1975 OSU 21, Michigan 14: Two Ohio State touchdowns in the last 3:08 send the Bucks to Pasadena for the fourth straight year.

1976 Michigan 22, OSU 0: Finally, a win for Bo in Columbus as Russell Davis and Rob Lytle combine to score three second-half TDs.

1977 Michigan 14, OSU 6: Rick Leach scores the clincher on a third quarter run, and Hayes takes a swing at a TV cameraman.

1978 Michigan 14, OSU 3: In the last Bo-Woody battle, U-M keeps Ohio State out of the end zone for the third straight year.

30 Wins, 2 Losses, 0 Bowls

From 1972 through '74, Michigan's record was 30–2–1. The Wolverines racked up a 21-game unbeaten streak, their longest in 25 years. With Dennis Franklin running the option, they outscored their opponents 918–200 over those three years. The defense amassed 11 shutouts, and no one scored more than 20 points against them.

Yet Michigan never went to a bowl game and never beat Ohio State. Both losses and the tie came against the Buckeyes, and that made all the difference. Because when the Ohio State game ended, all they could do was go back to class and wait for next year.

These teams played vintage Bo Schembechler football, as they rammed the ball between the tackles or off the option for four, five, six yards a crack. The 1972 offensive line, with Paul Seymour at tackle and Mike Hoban and Tom Coyle at the guards, was one of the best in Michigan history. Dave Brown, Randy Logan, and Don Dufek were outstanding defensive backs, and Dave Gallagher earned

It all came down to the kicking game when Michigan played Ohio State from 1971 to '74. The largest margin of victory in those low-scoring games was three points, and one game was a tie.

All-America honors at defensive tackle. Ed Shuttlesworth was a load and a half as a ball carrier and blocker at fullback. The critics shouted "dull and boring," but Bo couldn't have cared less.

The 10–10 tie with OSU in 1973, however, changed college football. It was a foregone conclusion that Michigan would get the vote of the Big Ten athletic directors to go to Pasadena because of the no-repeat rule (which was no longer official Big Ten policy but was considered a rule of thumb). Woody already had wished Bo well on the bowl trip. But Franklin had gone down with a separated shoulder during the game, and conference officials—not wanting to lose a fifth straight Rose Bowl—lobbied for OSU. Six of the ten ADs, including MSU's, voted for Ohio State.

Bo was furious, convinced he had been betrayed by the Big Ten. He was almost in tears when he told his players what had happened, and he was disgusted by the implied slight to Larry Cipa, his backup quarterback. The reaction was so volcanic that the Big Ten voted to change its policies and allow teams other than the champion to accept bowl bids. Michigan was the first to benefit, going to the Orange Bowl after the 1975 season. That ruling opened up the entire postseason picture, leading in time to the Bowl Championship Series.

Franklin's shoulder healed by New Year's Day, and photographers took pictures of him throwing a football in the snow near his Ohio home. It made no difference. Despite a 29–2–1 career record, he never played a down in a bowl.

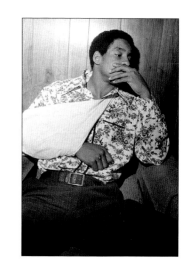

Because Dennis Franklin was injured, Big Ten officials felt that Michigan wouldn't be as competitive as Ohio State in the 1974 Rose Bowl. Thus, athletic directors voted that the Buckeyes go to Pasadena.

All-Americans of the '70s

Bo Schembechler said that when he got to Michigan, "the cupboard was not bare, thanks to Bump." Bo walked into a championship in the making. All it lacked was his imprint.

Schembechler's philosophy started and ended with the offensive line. Without that, he said, you had nothing because you couldn't control the ball and your defense wore down late in games. With Dan Dierdorf at tackle and Reggie McKenzie at guard, he had a line for the ages. Both would be enshrined in the College Football Hall of Fame.

Dierdorf, who grew up in Canton, Ohio, had been unsuccessfully recruited by Bo at Miami. He recalled in later years that when Bo arrived at Michigan, he greeted Dierdorf by saying, "You're fat, you're mine, and I never forget a slight." McKenzie, who was raised in the Detroit suburb of Highland Park, was regarded as one of the best pulling guards of the era. His devastating blocks on the Michigan trap enabled teams of the early '70s to erase every school rushing record.

Tailback Billy Taylor was another player who got away from Bo at Miami, which annoyed him all the more because he came from his hometown of Barberton, Ohio. Running behind a great offensive line, he became Michigan's all-time rushing leader in 1971. He also rebuilt his life in later years, with the support of Bo, after problems with drugs and the law. He eventually earned a doctorate in counseling.

Taylor's rushing records were surpassed by Rob Lytle, another Ohio product whom Woody dearly coveted. The All-American offensive linemen kept coming, too. Paul Seymour at tackle, Mark Donahue at guard, and Walt Downing at center.

Even more surprising was the development of Jim Smith, the first great wide receiver that Bo recruited. As a target for Rick Leach, and a terrific return specialist, he amassed 2,890 career all-purpose yards and gave the Wolverines a new dimension to their offense.

Fast and powerful, offensive tackle Dan Dierdorf earned consensus All-America honors in 1970. He was elected to both the College Football and Pro Football halls of fame.

Ferocious D

As good as the offense was during the 1970s, the swarming defenses designed primarily by assistant coaches Gary Moeller and Bill McCartney were even more intimidating. The Michigan defensive backs in this era made passing against the Wolverines a journey into fear. The wolfman position, which demanded speed and the ability to deliver bone-jarring hits, was turned into a Michigan signature by Randy Logan and Don Dufek, Jr. (son of the 1951 Rose Bowl hero).

Curtis Greer set a school career record with 48 tackles for loss from his tackle position. Linebacker Calvin O'Neal established a Michigan record with 378 career tackles, only to be surpassed by Ron Simpkins three years later. Six of these 1970s teams held opponents to fewer than 100 points in a season, led by the 1972 group, which surrendered a mere 57.

Bo's Generals

The Schembechler game plan did not involve recklessly throwing the football around. In fact, starting quarterback Rick Leach completed only 32 passes in 12 games in 1975. Only when Bo began to realize that the absence of Michigan quarterbacks on any roster in the NFL was hurting recruiting did he rethink the position.

Bo's QBs for his first three years, Don Moorhead and Tom Slade, were primarily runners whose job was to keep mistakes to a minimum and hand off to the running backs. While Dennis Franklin and Rick Leach were perfect for the option offense that Bo designed, their talents did not fit the professional mold. Nonetheless, in the seven years Franklin and Leach started at the position, Michigan's record was 68–10–3.

Leach was the first freshman quarterback ever to start for Michigan, and for four seasons no one could move him aside. Well, Bo did sit him in the third week of that first year (1975), but when it resulted in a tie with lowly Baylor, he never did it again. The Leach record: three Big Ten titles, three galling Rose Bowl losses, and a loss to the national champion Oklahoma team in the 1976 Orange Bowl.

Called the "guts and glue of the maize and blue," Leach amassed a 38–8–1 record. The left-handed option quarterback broke the NCAA career record for most touchdowns throwing and running combined (82), and he finished third in the Heisman voting his senior year. But when he turned pro it was as a baseball player, with the Detroit Tigers. While never a regular, he did play ten years in the majors, compiling a .268 career average.

As the game evolved, and especially after repeated disappointments against Pac-10 teams in the Rose Bowl, things started to change. The first genuine passing quarterback under Bo's regime was John Wangler, and that was kind of an accident. B. J. Dickey, who was more in the framework that Bo liked, went down with injuries in the Indiana game in 1979, and Wangler—who grew up in the Detroit suburb of Royal Oak—came in. His at-the-gun TD pass to freshman Anthony Carter won him the job, although Bo still didn't trust him to start against Ohio State that year.

Quarterback Rick Leach rushed for 2,717 yards in his career while averaging just five completed passes per game. Three times he was named All-Big Ten.

Bo was happy to have No. 9, Dennis Franklin, as his starting quarterback. Franklin exploded the racist myth that African American quarterbacks couldn't win, posting a career winning percentage of 92.2.

But why have an incredible talent like Carter if you couldn't get the ball to him? So Wangler was permitted to hit his stride in 1980, when the Wolverines went 10–2. Michigan came back from two early losses to win nine in a row, including Bo's first Rose Bowl win. Wangler was at the controls throughout the season.

Yet Bo, it seemed, could not bear to break with the past. His next quarterback, Steve Smith, was a three-year starter with a game much closer to Leach's. Smith's overall 25–10 record, although commendable, did not stack up with his predecessors. While Carter was still breaking records, it did not translate into the winning consistency of the past.

Jim Harbaugh, who literally grew up around the Michigan program as the son of an assistant coach (and was even used by Bo as a baby-sitter), was groomed for the quarterback job. He was a classic drop-back passer, and his season-ending injury five games into 1984 was a disaster. There was no Plan B, and the Wolverines lurched through a 6–6 year, the closest Bo ever came to a losing season.

But over the next two seasons, as the critics chorused that the game had passed Bo by, Harbaugh took Michigan to a 21–3–1 record, a No. 2 finish in the 1985 polls, and an impressive Fiesta Bowl triumph over Nebraska. He then went on to a professional career (primarily with Chicago and Indianapolis), becoming the first of Bo's QBs to make a mark in the NFL.

Harbaugh's replacement, Demetrius Brown, had both good and bad afternoons. He is remembered for his dramatic last-second TD pass to John Kolesar to win the Hall of Fame Bowl against Alabama after the 1987 season. Better yet, he engineered the win over Southern California the following year for Bo's second and final Rose Bowl title.

Scrambling Michael Taylor led Schembechler's last team to a 10–2 finish, but he couldn't win the Rose Bowl. Elvis Grbac, another drop-back passer, was waiting in the wings to take over under the new regime.

John Wangler posted a passer rating of 162.0 in 1979—a mark that no Michigan quarterback since has reached. He averaged a phenomenal 11.0 yards per passing attempt that season.

The Wolverines entered the 1977 Rose Bowl game leading the nation in both points scored (38.7) and fewest points allowed (7.2). Alas, they lost to Southern Cal, 14—6.

THE 1977 ROSE BOWL
USC vs. MICHIGAN

JANUARY 1 PASADENA, CALIFORNIA
official souvenir program $2

Rob Lytle, the Big Ten MVP and a consensus All-American in 1976, gets a hug after his one-yard touchdown run in the 1977 Rose Bowl.

Michigan and Ohio State fans taunted each other with bumper stickers. One Buckeye-hating sticker of the 1970s proclaimed: "You Go South Until You Smell It and Then East Until You Step in It."

OHOWIHATE OHIO STATE!

An Associated Press photographer captured Anthony Carter as he raced into the end zone to conclude the dramatic Michigan-Indiana game of 1979.

After opening 8–0 (with an average score of 44–8) in 1976, the "Sports Illustrated jinx" finally hit U-M when it lost to a mediocre Purdue team 16–14.

After not meeting for 35 years, Michigan and Notre Dame rekindled their rivalry in 1978. U-M won that season's game easily, 28–14, but suffered close, painful defeats to the Irish in '79 and '80.

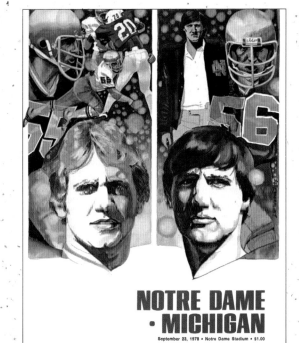

Michigan lost the 1979 Rose Bowl 17–10 to USC. Charles White's "phantom touchdown" was the difference.

New Year's Blues

Michigan's great run of top-ten finishes continued through the middle and late '70s under Rick Leach. Maddeningly, the record of failing to win the season's last game ran to 13 straight years. Only the 10–10 tie with Ohio State in 1973, even more frustrating in its own way, broke the chain of losses.

Despite whipping the Buckeyes in 1976, '77, and '78, Michigan endured frustrations each year. Upsets by Purdue and Minnesota ruined unbeaten regular seasons. The '76 Purdue game, a 16–14 stunner that Michigan lost when a last-minute field goal try sailed wide, knocked U-M out of the No. 1 ranking. So did the inexplicable 16–0 defeat at Minnesota the following year. It was the first time that Bo's Wolverines had ever been blanked.

Things were even gloomier in the bowls. The 14–6 loss in the 1976 Orange Bowl by a great Oklahoma team, with a defense sparked by the Selmon brothers, could be tolerated. To Bo, only the Rose Bowl really mattered. It was as if part of him was still a kid in snowy Ohio listening to the sun-drenched game over the radio. But Pasadena was not kind to him.

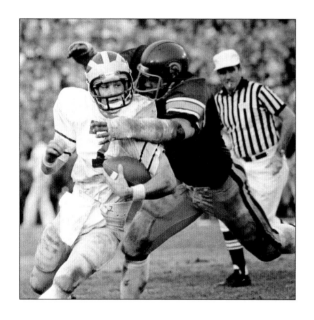

A four-year starter, quarterback Rick Leach lost only eight games in his career—but half of them were in bowl games, including the 1977 Rose Bowl (pictured).

Following the 1976 to '78 seasons, USC beat him twice and Washington once—all losses by the margin of a touchdown. The No. 2 ranking before the January 1977 game was the highest Bo ever had going to a bowl. But a Charles White TD with three minutes to play sealed the 14–6 Trojans win, although Michigan got as far as the 17 afterward.

More galling was a 27–20 loss to Washington the following year. The underdog Huskies behind Warren Moon ran off to a 24–0 third-quarter lead before a furious Leach-led comeback fell short on a goal-line interception off Stan Edwards's shoulder pad. Then in January 1979, Michigan lost another teeth-gnasher to USC by a 17–10 margin. Happy New Year, indeed!

USC's Phantom TD

Charles White's phantom touchdown was the difference in the 1979 Rose Bowl. Replays and photographs clearly showed that the USC tailback lost control of the football well outside the end zone on his three-yard score in the second quarter. Michigan recovered the fumble, but the line judge called it a TD. ESPN ranked it among the ten worst calls in sports history.

White's famous fumble

The major difference in all these games, though, was the ability of the Pac-10 teams to stifle Michigan's running attack. The Wolverines were usually outgained on the ground, and White ran for 213 yards by himself in the two USC games. Clearly, the game plan that smashed all Big Ten opposition was not carrying Michigan through the bowls.

Game Day

The great appeal of Michigan football is the way tradition is honored in an almost unchanging ritual. Pregame festivities include the entering of the stadium by the marching band; the first rendition of "The Victors" as the band comes roaring out of the north end zone; the songs they play and the Block M formation; and the team rushing out of the tunnel to leap up and touch the M Club banner. They are ingrained in the memory of every Michigan fan, and seeing them again after a long time away from Ann Arbor can bring tears to their eyes.

The early 1970s were a rambunctious age, however. Michigan made hash out of most opponents, and the games were decided rather early. To stem the boredom, students sometimes resorted to such pastimes as the infamous Pass 'Em Up and Look 'Em Over. This involved passing a female student overhead up through the stands of the student section. Security put a stop to this after a few years, as it was considered a safety risk and an insult to women. But for a few years, no young woman would dare attend games wearing anything other than pants.

There was also the announcement of the score of the Slippery Rock game. That always drew a round of applause, but it had to be discontinued when Michigan subscribed to a new score update service that only included "major" schools.

This was when the student section began taking out their keys and shaking them noisily whenever a "key" play was about to take place on the field. It also was the era in which massive tailgate parties in the parking lots surrounding the stadium became an essential part of the Michigan football experience.

Michigan Stadium also featured The Wave, which began during the 1983 season. The stadium-circling cheer had supposedly originated at the University of Washington and was adopted by fans of the Oakland A's baseball team. After seeing it at the Big House, fans of the Detroit Tigers picked it up, and it became a signature of their 1984 rush to the world championship. Henceforth, The Wave became the biggest fad in sports.

There were subtle variations, but a Michigan fan of the 1950s wouldn't have felt too far out of place on game day during the '80s. Nor has the scene changed perceptibly from that day to this. The Michigan brass has realized that they shouldn't mess with a good thing.

It's the moment Michigan fans look forward to before every game: when the Wolverines pour out of the tunnel and leap to touch the M Club banner.

Despite his curmudgeonly demeanor, fans loved Bo Schembechler—especially these nine Michigan crazies.

The Human Torpedo

Michigan always preaches the importance of the program over the individual. But if any single player changed the way Bo Schembechler coached at Ann Arbor, it would have to be Anthony Carter.

His skills as a receiver were so great that to eschew the passing game with Carter on the field would have been beyond stubborn. And whatever else can be said about him, Bo was not stuck on stupid.

Carter arrived on campus in 1979, a shy kid from Florida who got so homesick that he was ready to pack it in as a freshman and go back to the Sunshine State. Only a stern lecture from a family member persuaded him to return to Ann Arbor. His impact on Michigan football was profound, not only in changing offensive plans but in enlarging U-M's recruiting area to parts of the country it had previously ignored. It caused grumbling among the faculty, but Michigan was now committed to going into southern states to find talent in smaller communities.

Dubbed the "Human Torpedo" by Bob Ufer, Carter was impossible to cover one-on-one. And with John Wangler throwing to him during his first two seasons, Michigan finally had an offense that was multidimensional. Bo was enormously fond of the 160-pound Carter, and as a token

Carter was the ultimate big-play guy—as both a receiver and a kickoff and punt returner. His 17.4 yards per touch for his career established an NCAA record.

of his affection he gave him uniform No. 1. No special significance was attached to it previously, but after Carter it has been worn only by receivers the coaching staff deems worthy.

Carter never won a Heisman Trophy, but he did finish fourth (and won the Big Ten MVP Award) his senior year. He also shattered Michigan career records for pass receptions, TD catches, yards gained, and return yardage. His 33 career touchdown receptions were second best in NCAA history when he left in 1982. Moreover, he was Michigan's first three-time All-American since Bennie Oosterbaan in the 1920s.

AC's Electrifying Touchdown

Anthony Carter really arrived in the eighth game he played at Michigan, in 1979. The opponent was Indiana. Usually a conference doormat, the Hoosiers had put together a 5–2 record and were playing Michigan to a standstill at the Big House. With six seconds to go, the game tied 21–21, and U-M at Indiana's 45, quarterback John Wangler hit Carter over the middle. AC blew past three defenders and then shot into the end zone.

Carter celebrates the TD

The Michigan crowd went berserk, rushing the field and trying to tear down the goalposts. Bob Ufer screamed indecipherably into the microphone and blasted on his George Patton scoring horn. When Ufer came to his senses, he declared: "Johnny Wangler to Anthony Carter will be heard until another hundred years of Michigan football is played. I've never been so happy in all my cotton-pickin' 59 years!"

Carrying the Mail

Tailbacks thrived in Bo Schembechler's system. They could operate behind Michigan's massive offensive line—as well as behind a fullback who usually could knock opposing linebackers on their keisters. From Rob Lytle to Butch Woolfolk to Jamie Morris, great running backs were a Michigan staple throughout the '70s and '80s, with each one obliterating the records set by his predecessor.

Billy Taylor was actually Michigan's first star running back under Bo. After his departure and with Dennis Franklin directing the option attack, it was fullback Ed Shuttlesworth who carried the brunt of the Michigan running game. But with Lytle's arrival in 1974, the emphasis shifted.

In a recruiting coup, Bo snagged Lytle from right under Woody Hayes's nose in Ohio. Lytle, who was a bit over six feet and a bit under 200 pounds, never regretted the choice. "Those seasons playing for Bo were the best of my life," he said in a *Toledo Blade* interview. "I was playing

Tailback Jamie Morris employs his amazing cut-back ability to elude legendary Ohio State linebacker Chris Spielman. The waterbug tailback rushed for 210 yards against Ohio State in 1986.

for a guy I'd go to hell and back for, and I knew he would always go to war for you."

In 1976 Lytle won the Big Ten MVP Award and finished third in the Heisman balloting. He broke the Michigan career rushing record with 3,317 career yards before going on to play in a Super Bowl with the Denver Broncos.

Woolfolk came out of New Jersey, and in his freshman campaign of 1978 it was apparent that he was the tailback of the future. Stan Edwards had seemed to have a lock on that position. But in a decision that Schembechler always said was among the most selfless he ever saw, Edwards volunteered to move to fullback. That meant far fewer carries for him in a role that would be primarily as a blocking back for Woolfolk.

But it worked. Woolfolk's 92-yard run against Wisconsin in 1979 set a school record. He was named MVP of the 1981 Rose Bowl, was a consensus All-American, and bested Lytle's rushing record by 544 yards.

Then came Morris, whom Bo called the "cutest little running back in America." An indestructible 5'7" bundle from Massachusetts, Morris received a scholarship only after Michigan assistant coaches persuaded a reluctant Schembechler to give him a shot. Morris was almost hidden behind a huge line anchored by 6'7" Jumbo Elliott, and when he finished, his rushing mark of 4,393 yards (subsequently broken by Anthony Thomas) was yet another school record.

Running behind Michigan's massive, well-conditioned offensive line in the mid-1970s, Rob Lytle averaged 5.9 yards per carry for his career.

The Drought Ends

In 1980 it finally came together on the season's final day. Michigan's string of bowl losses, which had reached an embarrassing seven in a row—including one to North Carolina in the previous season's Gator Bowl—was gnawing at the gut of the Wolverines.

That 1979 team had finished 8–4 and dropped all the way to 18th in the final Associated Press poll, the first time Bo had finished out of the top ten at Michigan. The 1980 AP poll placed the Wolverines at No. 12. But Bo knew something the pollsters didn't. This team was loaded.

> **"I don't care if you have to force the throw. Just get the ball to Carter."**
>
> **Bo to quarterback John Wangler at the 1981 Rose Bowl**

With John Wangler throwing the ball, Anthony Carter catching it, Butch Woolfolk running, and an offensive line with four current or future All-Americans—Ed Muransky, Kurt Becker, Bubba Paris, and George Lilja—no one would stop them. Even better, the defense clicked thanks to a resolute bunch of role players led by linebacker Andy Cannavino.

It didn't seem that way at first. Two nonconference losses—to Notre Dame on a field goal on the last play of the game and, more shockingly, at home to South Carolina—shook the faith. Michigan dropped clear out of the polls, and Bo went back to the trenches with his staff. The team never lost again, and in the last five games of the season no one crossed its goal line. Over the last six games of the conference schedule, the Wolverines outscored the opposition 176–31.

Then it was another date in Pasadena with Washington as the opponent. This was the team that had beaten the Wolverines three years before. And just as in that Rose Bowl, Michigan was ranked far ahead of the Huskies. For 30 minutes it looked like the same familiar story, with the Wolverines clinging to a 7–6 lead. Following Bo's halftime instructions, however, Wangler opened up the offense. When he hit Carter on a seven-yard TD strike with three minutes left in the third quarter, the lead grew to 17–6 and the matter was settled.

Michigan moved the ball easily against Washington, amassing 437 yards of total offense. Woolfolk rushed for 182 yards and a touchdown. The final was 23–6, and an overjoyed Michigan team had given its coach the first bowl win of his career.

After losing his first seven bowl games, Bo Schembechler finally celebrated on New Year's Day, 1981. The Wolverines were ranked fourth in the season-ending AP poll.

Fighting the Irish

Bo didn't like the idea at all. He figured that two big emotional games were already on Michigan's schedule—Michigan State and Ohio State. He didn't relish adding a third with a nonconference matchup against a team like Notre Dame.

But he was in the minority. The two winningest big-time programs just *had* to get together again after a hiatus of 35 years. It was destiny. Besides, both schools knew a moneymaker when they saw one. So in 1978, the Wolverines went down to South Bend to pick up the old rivalry.

It couldn't have been better timing. The Irish were defending national champions, and although they had been upset in the opener by Missouri, this was still a

Gerald White celebrates his three-yard touchdown run against Notre Dame in 1985, a game won by Michigan 20–12. The series resumed that year after a two-year hiatus.

monumental quarterback matchup between Rick Leach and Joe Montana. Michigan came away with an impressive 28–14 win, and the series was on.

It would rarely be that easy again. The next nine times the teams met, Bo's Wolverines went 3–6. Six of those games were decided by six points or fewer, and three of them went down to the last minute. Unfortunately, the Irish won two of them. Not even the Buckeyes were that tough during this era.

From the standpoint of Michigan, the two most agonizing defeats came from the feet of Harry Oliver and Reggie Ho. Fans at Notre Dame Stadium still swear that the wind blowing in Oliver's face in the 1980 game abated just as he kicked the 51-yard field goal that won the game, 29–27, as time expired. In 1988 little Reggie Ho kicked four field goals, the last with 73 seconds left, to beat Michigan 19–17—a win that started an Irish run to the national championship.

But sometimes the Irish missed those kicks. Michigan and Jim Harbaugh knocked off Notre Dame 24–23 in 1986 when ND's field goal try from 45 yards out drifted wide in the last minute. It also helped that the Irish turned the ball over three times inside the Michigan 20.

The most satisfying Michigan win, however, was in 1981, when they dismantled the top-ranked Irish 25–7. What made it even sweeter was that the Wolverines had been upset by Wisconsin in the opener. Michigan players who thought they knew what an intense Schembechler practice was like realized they didn't have a clue during that week of preparation. The poor Irish never had a chance.

The Michigan football program celebrated its 100th anniversary in 1979. Its record entering the '79 season was 606–200–31.

Linebacker Ron Simpkins amassed a school-record 174 tackles in 1977. He broke U-M's career tackles record (516) in 1979, when he was named an All-American.

Gerald Ford (*left*) remained a loyal follower of Michigan football during his presidency and even attended Michigan practices.

Michigan's defense was impenetrable over the last 5½ games of the 1980 season. It did not allow a touchdown over that stretch, which included a 23–6 win over Washington in the Rose Bowl.

For four years, tackle John "Jumbo" Elliott (6'7", 306 pounds) blocked gaping holes for tiny Jamie Morris (5'7", 188), helping him breaking the Michigan record for career rushing yards.

With their win in the Fiesta Bowl, the Wolverines finished the 1985 season ranked No. 2 in the AP poll—the highest finish in Bo Schembechler's coaching career.

Whenever Michigan State has tried to assert its authority, Michigan seemingly has always come back to prove its dominance (at least on the football field!).

The Canham Touch

October 25, 1975. Mark the date. Michigan annihilated another dreadful Indiana team, 55–7, on that day to hold on to the seventh spot in the national rankings. A crowd of 93,857 turned out to witness the annihilation at Michigan Stadium.

Former Wolverine Gerald Ford was president. Elton John's "Island Girl" topped the pop charts. Cincinnati's Big Red Machine had just won its first World Series. And from that day to this, there practically has not been a seat to spare in the Big House.

It was the last time Michigan played before a home attendance of anything less than 100,000. Two weeks later,

An NCAA high jump champion in his younger days, Canham raised the bar as an athletic director. His marketing innovations helped the Michigan Athletic Department become the envy of the nation.

on November 8, Purdue was disposed of 28–0, and the streak of capacity crowds has been running ever since.

This was the fruit of Don Canham's labor. One of the authentic marketing geniuses in the history of sports, Michigan's athletic director turned U-M football from an easy ticket into solid gold.

During the 1968 World Series, Canham had a helicopter fly over Detroit's Tiger Stadium pulling banners that touted Michigan football. Canham reasoned that's where the sports fans were, and each one of them was a potential customer.

Canham sold the sizzle as well as the steak. Game day was more than football, he preached. It included the tailgating and the fun of spending a glorious autumn afternoon in one of America's most picturesque college towns. He sent out random flyers in the mail, and he hawked Michigan tickets to not just alumni but people who may never have entered a college classroom. If you sell it, they will come. And Canham knew selling.

Like Bob Ufer, Canham had been a track and field star at Michigan, winning an NCAA title in the high jump. He went on to coach the track team for 20 years while launching a successful company that sold track equipment and other products. He was a wealthy man by 1968 when he accepted the offer to become athletic director.

Job one was to fill the enormous number of empty seats. Since the stadium had expanded capacity to 101,001 in 1956, it had reached that number only seven times, and in every instance it was for the Michigan State game. Its attendance regularly lagged far behind that of Ohio State,

It killed Canham to see more than 24,000 empty seats for Michigan's home opener in 1974. After October 1975 (to the present day), the stadium has been packed for every game.

which had 15,000 fewer seats to sell. Michigan had to resort to freebie programs like an annual Band Day to get people into the stadium.

Even during an 8–2 season in 1968, average attendance was below 70,000. That figure was great for most programs, and it was never worse than fifth in the country. But Canham hated to keep excess inventory on his hands. It took him seven years, and the masterstroke of hiring Bo Schembechler, before he filled all those seats. It also helped that from the Missouri game of 1969 to the Ohio State game of 1975—a run of 41 home Saturdays—Michigan did not lose in the Big House.

Canham also grew the stadium by slow and steady increments. Railings were removed, allowing for an extra row of seats, and a few boxes were replaced with bleachers. By the end of the 1980s, capacity exceeded 106,000, and a record crowd of 106,137 turned out for the Ohio State game of 1989. Canham had aroused the sleeping giant that was Michigan football in the 1950s and '60s, turning it into the behemoth of today.

Canham's Carpet

One of the most controversial moves Canham made was to carpet Michigan Stadium with Tartan Turf before the 1969 season. The rationale was that it required less upkeep and would not turn to mush in bad weather. The downside was that it was a harder, more dangerous surface for the players—and a distinct break with tradition.

The initial outlay of the artificial surface was $250,000. When the decision was made to go back to grass in 1991, the cost of resodding was nearly ten times that much. As a bonus, however, the playing field was lowered by more than three feet, improving sight lines. Moreover, two full rows of seats were added all the way around the stadium.

'80s Recession

You can keep eight other teams down for only so long. In the early 1980s, the downtrodden doormats of the Big Ten began catching up to Michigan. With Hayden Fry running the Iowa program and Mike White coaching at Illinois, the Wolverines and Buckeyes now had strong and persistent challengers.

Iowa came into the Big House in 1981 and stymied a powerful Michigan offense, winning 9–7. It was the first time the Hawkeyes had won at Michigan in 33 years, and the first time they had beaten them anywhere since 1962. Fry became an irritant to Bo later in the decade when he insisted on painting the visiting locker room pink at Kinnick Stadium. Fry felt it pacified Iowa's opponents. It was doubly exasperating when Michigan lost there twice in a row. On the next trip in, Bo put up paper to conceal the paint.

His anger toward Illinois was more serious. Bo felt that his longtime assistant, Gary Moeller, had been given a bum deal there, getting fired just as his recruiting efforts were about to pay off. Worse yet in Bo's mind, Moeller's replacement, White, was using a lot of junior college transfers. His rage at losing to the Illini in 1983 by a 16–6 score was boundless, especially since it sent them to the Rose Bowl.

Bo did sneak in another trip to Pasadena with the 1982 team, but it was far from vintage Michigan. The Wolverines finished 8–4, lost both nonconference games and to Ohio State, gave up an unacceptable 204 points (worst of the entire Schembechler era), and were drubbed in the Rose Bowl by UCLA 24–14. It was Michigan's second loss

to the Bruins that season, and U-M was not ranked in the final AP poll for the first time under Bo.

Worse was yet to come. In 1984 an injury to Jim Harbaugh left Michigan without a top-caliber quarterback. The injury-riddled team staggered through a 6–5 regular season and finished sixth in the conference. Iowa clobbered U-M 26–0, the worst loss of Bo's career at Michigan. The Wolverines went to the Holiday Bowl to play Brigham Young, and they gave the eventual national champions a tough game before losing in the last two minutes, 24–17.

The game had passed Bo by, crowed the critics. But that obituary, as it turned out, was a bit premature.

Michigan held star running back Alonzo Highsmith in check in the 1984 season opener, in which U-M defeated reigning national champion Miami 22–14. However, the Wolverines' season unraveled due to injuries, and they finished at 6–6.

Tears Rain in East Lansing

In recent decades, it has not taken long for a Michigan State coach to become frustrated after arriving in East Lansing. After MSU dominated Michigan for two decades, the balance switched emphatically in 1970. For the last 20 years of Bo Schembechler's tenure, he was 17–3 against the Spartans.

When Michigan State cast its vote against Michigan for the Rose Bowl berth in 1973—sending Ohio State to Pasadena—Schembechler swore to exact revenge, which he did repeatedly. In most years, it wasn't even close. Michigan's average margin of victory was 17 points, and four of those triumphs came by shutouts.

More than bragging rights and the Paul Bunyan Trophy were at stake. The teams competed in recruiting over the same territory, and Michigan's return to national prominence swung the choice of many talented young athletes throughout the Midwest. In 1980 Spartans head coach Darryl Rogers left for Arizona State in frustration after he realized he could not match up in this battle.

Even when State arose and smote the Wolverines, something usually marred the celebration. When Rogers smacked down his "arrogant" tormentors in 1978 by a 24–15 score in Ann Arbor and then tied for the Big Ten championship, the team was on probation and missed out on the Pasadena trip. Who went in their place? The co-champion, Michigan.

Michigan State coach Darryl Rogers fueled the intrastate rivalry in 1978 when he referred to U M supporters as "arrogant asses."

Massive defensive end Kevin Brooks (6'6", 273 pounds) prepares to devour the Michigan State quarterback in the 1983 game, which the Wolverines won 42–0.

Not until George Perles arrived in 1983 did State begin to establish a kind of parity. After enduring a 42–0 beating in his first year, Perles upended Michigan 19–7 the following season. But that was the year that six teams beat Michigan. A far sweeter victory came in 1987, when Perles drubbed the Wolverines 17–11 and took MSU to the Rose Bowl for the first time in 22 years. He became the first State coach since Duffy Daugherty to beat the Wolverines twice.

Michigan's rivalry with Ohio State was bitter, but this internal feud had a nastier edge to it. More major penalties were called in these games than when Michigan played the Buckeyes, and shoving in the tunnel from the locker rooms could sometimes lead to further unpleasantness. It seemed to grow even worse in later years, when uncalled penalties and a slow clock in 2001 infuriated the Maize and Blue.

Buckeye Battles

Many predicted that the annual Michigan-Ohio State game would lose some of its luster after Woody Hayes was forced into retirement. Not a huge amount, but maybe just enough to let you know that the Ten-Year War was over. But Woody's replacement, Earle Bruce, knew the drill. Taking over after three straight losses to the Wolverines, he fully understood what was expected of him in 1979.

Just like the historic meeting in 1969, the '79 matchup featured a revered icon against a new guy. Only this time the roles were reversed, with Bruce as the new coach vowing to end a disturbing string of losses to the hated enemy.

Though the Buckeyes entered the game at 10–0, they hadn't scored a touchdown on Michigan since 1975, and the string continued for two more quarters. A 59-yard John Wangler to Anthony Carter strike had Michigan up 7–6 at the half. But this time Ohio State had a fancy passer of its own in Art Schlichter. He threw a scoring pass in the third quarter that seemed to break the spell. It took a blocked punt and recovery for a touchdown to do it, but Bruce won the first encounter 18–15.

Still, the everything-is-on-the-table atmosphere that defined these games from 1968 to 1979 slowly dissipated. There was no longer a conference title and trip to the Rose Bowl at stake every November. Iowa, Illinois, and Michigan State grabbed that ring four times during the decade of the '80s, and in 1987 neither team was ranked in the AP

The Buckeyes focused on tailback Butch Woolfolk (pictured) in the 1981 game. The senior speedster, who won numerous Big Ten track championships, broke the Michigan career rushing record in '81.

top 20 when they met. That hadn't happened in 20 years, and it had been regarded as unthinkable on both sides of the border.

Bruce had a good run, even eking out a 5–4 margin over Bo in their meetings. He took the Buckeyes to a bowl every year except for one. Unfortunately for him, it was the Rose Bowl only twice, and both of those visits ended in a defeat. He lost only 23 regular-season games in his nine years on the job. But after the glory years with Woody, nothing short of a title every season was going to be good enough in Columbus.

When he slipped to a 6–4–1 mark in 1987, Bruce was canned. The boom was lowered just before the Michigan game, and a fired-up Ohio State team upset the Wolverines 23–20. Schembechler, who had coached with Bruce on Woody Hayes's staff, respected him. Bo said afterward

Ohio State coach Earle Bruce, who was fired just before the 1987 OSU-Michigan game, coached that contest and wound up beating his nemesis 23–20.

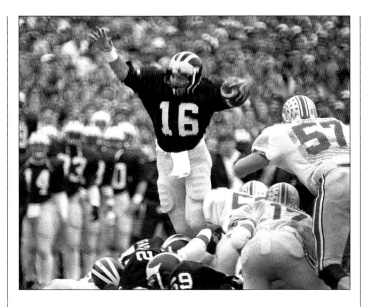

Quarterback Steve Smith, who lost two straight games to Ohio State, finally prevailed as a senior in 1983, the year he was named team MVP.

that "this was one time I didn't mind losing to Ohio State so much," and he sunk the barb in by adding that Ohio State didn't know what it had with him as its coach.

The Buckeyes thought they knew just the man they wanted for a replacement: Arizona State's John Cooper. ASU had beaten Michigan 22–15 in the 1987 Rose Bowl. More than that, the Sun Devils actually had outmuscled the Wolverines, rare for a Pac-10 team, to come from behind in the second half. Cooper seemed to be a perfect fit. That turned out to be a miscalculation. Bo knocked him off twice before retiring as coach, and it took Cooper six tries before he could claim his first victory over Michigan.

All in all, Bo finished 6–5 against OSU in the post-Woody era and 11–9–1 versus the Buckeyes over his entire career. But no matter who was running the show on the opposite sideline, it was never easy.

U-M 6, OSU 5

1979 Ohio State 18, Michigan 15: A blocked punt and return gives the Buckeyes the win and a trip to Pasadena.

1980 Michigan 9, Ohio State 3: A John Wangler to Anthony Carter 13 yard TD pass propels U-M to Pasadena, where Bo enjoys his first Rose Bowl victory.

1981 Ohio State 14, Michigan 9: Art Schlichter's TD run with less than three minutes to play clinches the win.

1982 Ohio State 24, Michigan 14: Though the Wolverines have already clinched the Rose Bowl trip, they lose this game due to six turnovers.

1983 Michigan 24, Ohio State 21: U-M wins this seesaw battle thanks to a touchdown pass from Steve Smith to tight end Eric Kattus. Michigan goes to the Sugar Bowl.

1984 Ohio State 21, Michigan 6: A decisive thrashing of Bo's weakest team sends OSU to Pasadena. Keith Byars scores all three TDs for the Bucks.

1985 Michigan 27, Ohio State 17: In this rare air show, Jim Harbaugh fires three TD passes, including a 77-yarder to John Kolesar. Michigan goes to the Fiesta Bowl and Iowa prepares for Pasadena.

1986 Michigan 26, Ohio State 24: Jim Harbaugh guarantees victory, but U-M survives only because OSU misses a 45-yard field goal with 62 seconds left. Jamie Morris rushes for 210 yards, and Michigan goes to the Rose Bowl.

1987 Ohio State 23, Michigan 20: In Earle Bruce's swan song, Matt Franz nails a game-winning field goal.

1988 Michigan 34, Ohio State 31: Michigan blows a 20–0 halftime lead, but John Kolesar's heroics in the final two minutes (59-yard kickoff return; TD catch) win it for Michigan.

1989 Michigan 28, Ohio State 18: An overpowering ground game, with Jarrod Bunch scoring two TDs, sends Bo to the Rose Bowl in his final season.

MAXIMUM

THE BEST OF
Bob Ufer
DOUBLE CD SET

Never-before
heard cuts
from the
U of M Football
broadcast legend

MEECHIGAN

No one effused enthusiasm like Michigan broadcaster Bob Ufer. "He went down that Tartan Turf," he'd say after a particularly inspired run, "like a penguin with a hot herring in his cummerbund!"

1985 · 1986 · 1987 · 1988

JOHN KOLESAR

WIDE RECEIVER

Ufer honked his Bo "George Patton" Schembechler scoring horn whenever Michigan scored. A touchdown was worth three honks, a field goal two, and an extra point one.

Fans recall receiver John Kolesar for his late heroics against Ohio State in 1985 and '88—and his game-winning catch in the 1988 Hall of Fame Bowl.

'M' win is a heartfelt one for Bo

The Schef's Specialty
BY ADAM SCHEFTER

PASADENA, Calif. — The maize and blue helmets were raised to the sky, the...

Michigan coach Bo Schembechler hoists over his head his second Rose Bowl trophy. After three previous losses to Southern Cal in Pasadena, Schembechler...

See Victors, Page 7

Michigan Daily sports editor Adam Schefter comments on the 1989 Rose Bowl. Schefter eventually would join fellow Daily staffer Rich Eisen on the NFL Network.

Detroit Free Press sports columnist Mitch Albom authored his first book, *Bo*, eight years before his mammoth bestseller, *Tuesdays with Morrie.*

Life, laughs, and lessons of a college football legend

BO

BO SCHEMBECHLER & MITCH ALBOM

Michigan trailed USC 14–3 at the half of the 1989 Rose Bowl. But Bo stuck with his ground game and eventually wore down the Trojans, resulting in a 22–14 Michigan win.

Bo Schembechler amassed more rings than he had fingers in his 21 years as head coach, during which he won 13 Big Ten championships.

New Year's Fiesta

Although it did not end up in the Rose Bowl, the 1985 Michigan team was Bo's best during the '80s. More than that, it was a satisfying comeback from the disastrous 6–6 campaign of 1984, when his epitaph was being written across the Big Ten.

Michigan's punishing defense was anchored by tackle Mike Hammerstein and linebacker Mike Mallory. This unit ranked right alongside Michigan's great defensive teams of the 1970s. It held every regular-season opponent to 17 points or fewer, and its only loss (12–10 to Iowa) came on four field goals, the last one on the final play of the game. U-M also played Illinois to a 3–3 tie.

This was the first Michigan team to play before capacity crowds both at home and away, an indication of how balanced the Big Ten had become in this decade. Most of all, it was an entertaining team. Jim Harbaugh established himself as the best drop-back passer in Wolverines history. He shattered all school passing records and led the nation in passing efficiency. Michigan ran off a 15-game unbeaten streak in 1985–86, their longest since 1973–74.

Passing was fine, but Harbaugh also knew how to utilize the running of Jamie Morris and to seize the opportunities the defense gave him. That was on display in the Fiesta Bowl. Michigan drew a powerful Nebraska team, which had gone 9–2 and averaged 36 points a game. The Huskers hit Michigan with two second-quarter touchdowns and held a 14–3 halftime lead.

Then the defense went to work, forcing a fumble on the third play of the second half. Gerald White took it in from there. On the next series, Michigan recovered another

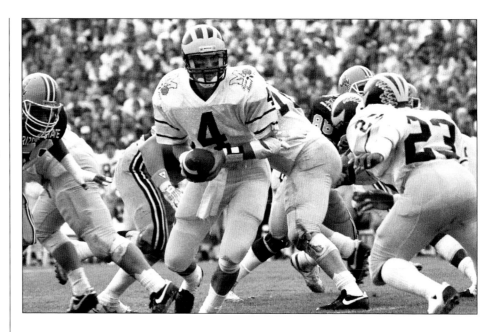

fumble in Nebraska territory. White ran for 19 yards, and Harbaugh scored himself. Just like that, the game had turned and Michigan was in front.

But the Wolverines weren't finished. Dave Arnold blocked a Nebraska punt, and Pat Moons kicked his second field goal. As soon as Michigan got the ball back, they drove in again, with Harbaugh scoring his second touchdown. Nebraska had been slapped with 24 straight points in ten minutes of action.

The defense forced four Nebraska turnovers. The Huskers made it close with nine points in the final quarter—two of them on a deliberate safety by Michigan—but the Wolverines won 27–23. They ended the season ranked No. 2 in the AP poll (behind Oklahoma), the highest finish ever for a Schembechler team.

Jim Harbaugh set Michigan passing records across the board in 1985, including completions, yards, and touchdowns. His heroics in the Fiesta Bowl keyed a 27–23 Wolverines victory.

Back Home in Pasadena

The scent of roses seems sweeter the longer you're away. In 1986 the Wolverines hadn't been to the Rose Bowl in four years. They had made trips to the Sugar, Holiday, and Fiesta bowls, but they just weren't the same.

The separation anxiety ended when Jim Harbaugh led Michigan to an 11–1 campaign in 1986 and a date with Arizona State. The defense couldn't quite match its performance of the previous year, but the Michigan offense rolled up double digits in every game. Only a last-second Minnesota field goal the week before the Ohio State game spoiled a perfect season. It should be noted, however, that Michigan had stayed unbeaten thanks to a last-gasp boot against Iowa four weeks earlier.

This team was loaded with talented receivers. John Kolesar and Greg McMurtry, who would inherit the coveted No. 1 jersey, were chief among them. Jamie Morris was in his junior year at tailback, and the big, fast offensive line exceeded even Schembechler's standards.

But the Sun Devils, playing in their first Rose Bowl, had their number. Coming back from a 15–3 deficit in the second quarter, Arizona State pummeled the defense with 19 straight points while neutralizing Harbaugh and Morris. The end result: a 22–15 rubout.

The offensive talent remained in 1987, but with Harbaugh gone Michigan sometimes had a hard time marching to the end zone. Notre Dame decisively beat Michigan in the opener, 26–7, and the Wolverines lost close conference tilts to Michigan State, Ohio State, and Indiana. It was the first time the Hoosiers defeated Michigan since their own Rose Bowl year in 1967.

The end result was 7–4, a trip to the Hall of Fame Bowl in Tampa, and a first-ever meeting with Alabama. But Bo wasn't there. He had to undergo quadruple bypass surgery in December. Eighteen years after his first coronary episode, it was apparent that his days in one of the most stressful jobs in sports were running out.

Offensive coordinator Gary Moeller ran the team, and with 50 seconds to play he found himself trailing 24–21. He was close enough for a tying field goal, but on fourth and three he decided to go for it. Demetrius Brown fired a pass to Kolesar, who grabbed it in the back corner of the end zone. Michigan prevailed 28–24 for one of its most dramatic bowl victories ever. However, Bo's surgery overshadowed everything else.

Running back Bob Perryman loses the ball and almost his head after being face-masked by Arizona State's Stacy Harvey in the 1987 Rose Bowl. Michigan recovered the ball but lost the game, 22–15.

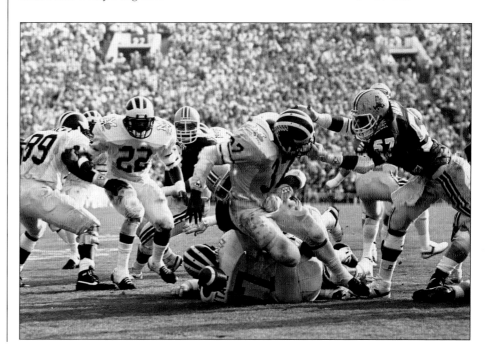

Stars of the '80s

The 1985 Wolverines yielded just 8.1 points per game—largely because of tackle Mike Hammerstein. He tied a school record that year with 23 tackles for loss.

While such stars as Anthony Carter, Jamie Morris, and Jim Harbaugh grabbed the headlines during the 1980s, Michigan was also developing some of its best linemen ever—on both sides of the ball.

The pressure Mike Hammerstein could put on opposing passers from his tackle position was a major reason the 1985 defensive unit was so dominating. He tied a school season record for tackles for losses, and he finished up by keying the big victory over Nebraska in the Fiesta Bowl. He was another of the gems plucked from Ohio, hailing from Wapakoneta.

His partner at tackle, Mark "Mess 'Em Up" Messner, eventually made his mark on the Michigan record book. He accumulated 70 tackles for losses during his career and led the team in sacks for four straight years. They were regarded as the most devastating combination of interior linemen ever to play on the Michigan defense. Linebacker Mike Mallory and defensive back Brad Cochran were All-Big Ten selections on the 1985 defensive unit, which allowed just eight points a game

Meanwhile, that '85 offense averaged 28.5 points a game, and tackle Jumbo Elliott was the paradigm of the offensive lineman Schembechler wanted. His 6'7", 306-pound frame made him one of the biggest linemen ever to play for the Wolverines. But it was his quickness and ability to open holes—through which Jamie Morris could scoot—that helped Michigan march downfield. He was especially effective against Alabama in the 1988 Hall of Fame Bowl, when Morris rushed for 234 yards.

Tom Dixon was another in the long line of great Michigan centers. He grew up in Indiana and wanted nothing more than to play for Notre Dame. But when the Irish failed to recruit him, Dixon fell into Michigan's lap. He spent his career opening holes for Michigan's running backs in the early '80s.

Tight end Eric Kattus was regarded as the best at that position during the Schembechler era. His combination of blocking and pass-catching talents were an integral part of the Harbaugh aerial attack in 1985.

Tripp Welborne was the last great safety developed by Bo. Although recruited by Michigan as a wide receiver, he made the switch effectively. In addition, he used his catching and running abilities to become the top punt return man on the 1989 Big Ten champions.

A quick, explosive defensive tackle, Mark Messner racked up 36 sacks in his Michigan career, shattering the school record by 17.

Bo Steps Down

When Bo made up his mind that it was time to leave, he came about as close as anyone could to going out on top. His last two teams won outright Big Ten championships, the first time that had happened since Michigan State did it in 1965–66. The Wolverines were 15–0–1 in the conference, and only a tie with Iowa in 1988 prevented the clean sweep.

Best of all, in January 1989 Bo achieved his second Rose Bowl victory—and his first in four tries against his New Year's nemesis, Southern California. This time it was a solid 22–14 victory, with Leroy Hoard rushing for 142 yards and two TDs. The fifth-ranked Trojans led 14–3 at the half before being shut down completely.

Michigan finished that '88 season 9–2–1, with last-minute losses to national champion Notre Dame and Miami. Those defeats came in the first two games of the season, and the Wolverines didn't crack the top ten again until after their Rose Bowl win, finishing at No. 4.

Bo's last game, on New Year's Day, 1990, was a Pasadena rematch. Ironically, it was one of his best chances at winning that elusive national title. A Michigan win combined with losses by Notre Dame and Miami in their bowl games would have done it. Unfortunately, none of it came off. Bo went off the stage with a 17–10 loss to Southern California.

The last lingering televised image of Bo showed him all tangled up in phone wires along the sidelines as he vigorously protested a penalty on a fake punt. The trick play had worked for a Michigan first down, but a holding penalty (which the films indicated was phantom) and an

Schembechler savors his last Rose Bowl victory, on January 1, 1989. One year later in Pasadena, in his final game before retirement, a bad call killed his chance of going out on top.

unsportsmanlike conduct flag on Bo turned the game. USC gathered in the subsequent punt and drove in for the winner with 70 seconds to play. But Bo went out battling, and that's what the man stood for.

Bo's Greatest Feats

What was Bo Schembechler's greatest accomplishment? The short answer is that he restored the Michigan program to the elite level. His philosophy continued to permeate the way the team prepared and played—carried on through the successors he trained, Gary Moeller and Lloyd Carr.

But if you need hard stats, try these: His 194 wins (against only 48 losses and five ties) were the most ever by a Michigan coach. He won 13 conference titles in his 21-year tenure. All 17 of his teams that were eligible went to a bowl. He never had a losing season. His 96–10–3 mark in the 1970s regular season was the best in the country. Sixteen of his teams finished in the AP top ten. And when he retired, his 234 career wins were the fifth most ever in Division I-A football.

Charles Woodson skies for an interception in the first half of the 1998 Rose Bowl. Michigan beat Washington State 21–16 to win a share of the national championship.

Perennial Power

1990–2007

After Bo Schembechler rebuilt Michigan's engine, Gary Moeller and Lloyd Carr kept the motor running. The Wolverines went undefeated in 1997 and eventually stretched their streak of consecutive non-losing seasons to 40—best in the nation.

Left: Sports Illustrated hailed Desmond Howard and Michigan after their stirring win over Notre Dame in 1991. Right: Lloyd Carr took over as head coach in 1995 and won a national title two years later.

From Bo to Moe

At first it seemed that only the first letter had changed. When Moe replaced Bo, Michigan barely missed a beat. In Gary Moeller's first three years, the Wolverines won three more Big Ten titles. That gave them five straight first-place finishes and a cumulative conference record of 35–2–3.

With Elvis Grbac throwing, Desmond Howard catching, and Tyrone Wheatley running, the Michigan offense was as devastating as ever. The 1990 Wolverines lost just two Big Ten games—by a total of two points.

The 431 points racked up by the 1992 touchdown machine came within one point of the best mark ever achieved by Bo. Michigan went 9–0–3 that year.

Moeller also had served under Woody Hayes at Ohio State, as a player and a captain of the 1961 team (although Hayes refused to autograph a book for him while he was an assistant at Michigan). He had been with Schembechler from before the beginning, as an assistant coach at Miami of Ohio and then—apart from three years as the head coach at Illinois—in Ann Arbor. He was as steeped as anyone in the Schembechler methodology and the Michigan tradition.

He also shared Bo's intensity. But unlike his mentor, Moeller was unable to let go of the disappointments and ignore the criticism. When the program hit some bumps in 1993 and 1994, he had coping problems. It had been an incredible run for the Wolverines, but with Big Ten com-

> "I can't be like Bo; that's not me. I think I have a longer point to where I boil, but when I get mad I stay mad."
>
> **Gary Moeller**

Moeller (left) proved he was just as effective as the great Lou Holtz (right). In Moe's five meetings against Holtz's Fighting Irish, he won two and tied one.

petition balanced once more—especially with the addition of Penn State—some readjustments were inevitable.

Three late losses at home during those two years, including bitter losses to Colorado and Penn State, gnawed at Moeller. During an evening out with his wife in April 1995, it came spilling out. A tirade in a restaurant fueled by alcohol and stress was caught on police tape recorders—then replayed mercilessly on radio over the next few days. Moeller was forced to resign, and with little advance preparation Lloyd Carr was named Michigan's interim head coach.

Moeller's overall record was a sparkling 44–13–3, including a Rose Bowl win after the 1992 season. He put together three straight top-ten finishes and a 3–1–1 record in the all-important Ohio State game. But his five-year tenure was the shortest at Michigan since Tad Wieman left after two seasons in 1928. One of the most pressure-packed jobs in football had to be passed on.

Blue vs. Gold

Notre Dame football went into a bit of a funk with the departure of Lou Holtz after the 1996 season, and the Irish struggled to find their identity over the following decade. However, you never would have known it from their series against Michigan. In the 13 games the two winningest programs in college football played against each other from 1990 through 2006, they finished 6–6–1. Michigan broke the tie in 2007, the year in which Notre Dame finished at 3–9.

The series was solidified as one of the great college rivalries during the 1990s. In fact, the total points dividing the teams in that decade was one (182–181, advantage Notre Dame). From 2002 on, Michigan made it a point to rearrange its schedule and get in a warm-up game so as not to open the season against the Irish. The game had become too big and too vital in the national rankings to enter it cold.

The high point for Michigan in an otherwise drab 1994 season was a 26–24 upset in South Bend. After falling behind 24–23, Todd Collins took Michigan 59 yards in the final 46 seconds. Remy Hamilton then kicked his fourth field goal of the game, from 42 yards out, to win it with two ticks on the clock. The clutch kick earned Hamilton national attention, and he became the first Michigan placekicker to be named an All-American.

For Michigan, it was payback for the 28–24 loss in 1990, when the Irish scored the winner with just 1:40 to go. Just as painful was the 17–17 tie in 1992 when Michigan lost a ten-point lead in the fourth quarter. Quarterback Elvis Grbac threw a pick just as the Wolverines were driving for a winning field goal.

It took second half heroics by Brian Griese and receiver Tai Streets to bring Michigan back from a halftime deficit against the Irish in 1997 and keep the undefeated season going. But with quarterback Jarious Jackson running the option the next year, Notre Dame ended the Wolverines' 12-game win streak with a severe 36–20 pummeling.

A 25–23 win over Michigan in 2002 gave rookie coach Ty Willingham instant credibility, as did a hotly disputed 17–10 victory in 2005 for his replacement, Charlie Weis. But the Wolverines didn't have to wait long for revenge. They blasted the Irish 38–0 in 2003 and then dismantled Weis's supposed title contenders 47–21 in 2006. In 2007, the same year in which the series was extended through 2031, both teams met with 0–2 records. Michigan avoided further embarrassment by whipping the Irish 38–0, with Mike Hart rushing for 187 yards.

Notre Dame receiver David Grimes and Michigan cornerback Leon Hall give their all for the ball in the 2006 game, won by Michigan 47–21.

Howard Hauls in the Heisman

Howard's sure hands, dazzling moves, and 23 TDs secured him the 1991 Heisman Trophy. He earned 640 first-place votes, 611 more than anyone else.

Desmond Howard provided two of the most memorable images in Michigan's history during his 1991 season. The first came in the Notre Dame game. The Irish had knocked off Michigan four straight years during a string of otherwise successful seasons for the Wolverines. Now they were threatening to do it again, coming back late in the game after Michigan had jumped off to an early lead. U-M's advantage was down to 17–14, and the Wolverines faced fourth and inches deep in Notre Dame territory.

Instead of the anticipated run, Elvis Grbac floated a pass into the back corner of the end zone. It seemed impossible that Howard could catch up to it, even though he had outdistanced the coverage. But he stretched out his 5'9" frame in a fully extended horizontal leap and came down cradling the ball. Howard's touchdown ended the Notre Dame comeback.

With a national television audience looking on, it was the catch that propelled Howard to the Heisman Trophy. Just to make sure, though, he saved one more big moment for Ohio State. During a 31–3 thrashing of the Buckeyes before an ecstatic Big House crowd, he returned a punt 93 yards. As he turned in the end zone, Desmond struck the pose of the player on the trophy. Who could deny him?

Howard was the first Michigan player in 51 years, since Tom Harmon, to win the award. He not only won it, he buried the opposition. According to Heisman records, he racked up the second largest margin of victory at that time, leading the balloting in every section of the country.

Howard became the first wide receiver ever to lead the run-oriented Big Ten in scoring. Besides his 15 touchdowns in conference games, he added eight more in four non-Big Ten games. He set 12 single-season Michigan records, including 19 straight games with a TD catch.

Even Anthony Carter hadn't completely buried the image of Michigan as a team that wanted to run first. But Howard did.

Record Smasher

For a traditionally conservative team, Desmond Howard's 1991 statistics popped off the page. In 12 games, he caught 62 passes for 985 yards and a whopping 19 touchdowns. His 13 rushes resulted in 180 yards (13.8 per carry) and two scores. He returned 15 kickoffs for 412 yards (27.5 average) and one touchdown, and he brought back 18 punts for 282 yards (15.7 average) and another TD. All told, he scored 23 touchdowns and led the Big Ten in scoring with 138 points. Howard finished the season (his third and last) with 37 career touchdowns.

Even though Michigan, unlike many other schools, traditionally does not campaign for Heisman awards, it was pretty much a foregone conclusion that the trophy was Howard's. His decision to turn pro was never in doubt, and while his success in the NFL never reached his college level, he was named MVP of Super Bowl XXXI with the Green Bay Packers.

Howard makes the catch that would clinch Michigan's victory over Notre Dame in 1991 and make him the front-runner for that season's Heisman Trophy.

Rockin' with Elvis

New Michigan coach Gary Moeller opened up the offense, allowing quarterback Elvis Grbac to surpass the Michigan career passing record by more than 1,000 yards.

It sometimes happens that two players from the same high school wind up on the same college team. But only on rare occasions does a quarterback-receiver combination continue its air show in Division I-A football.

Elvis Grbac and Desmond Howard both came out of little St. Joseph High, in the northeastern corner of Cleveland. A small school but formidable in football, St. Joseph also turned out NFL lineman Mike Golic and pro linebacker London Fletcher.

Grbac and Howard graduated high school in 1988 and made their way together to Ann Arbor. The Wolverines were hot on Howard's trail from the start, but they found Grbac by accident. He hadn't even played football until his junior year at St. Joseph. He came from a strict Croatian family, and his mother didn't like all that contact. But by his senior year, he was the starting quarterback. And when Gary Moeller visited to scout Howard, he came away sold on Grbac, too.

The arrival of this pair changed everything. From

With their win over Washington in the Rose Bowl, Michigan finished the 1992 season undefeated. Unfortunately, three ties—to Notre Dame, Illinois, and Ohio State—doomed them to a No. 5 finish in the AP and coaches polls.

the time Grbac took over the starter's job in 1990, the option attack was yesterday's news. Michigan now was committed to the drop-back quarterback as the critical component in its offense.

A steady stream of passing talent followed Elvis to Ann Arbor, all in pretty much the same mold: tall and not terribly fast. Todd Collins, Tom Brady, John Navarre, Chad Henne, and other disciplined gunslingers would follow in Grbac's footsteps. Many of the records he compiled would be subsequently erased.

Grbac won all four games he started as a freshman in 1989, and he went on to lead Division I-A in passing efficiency in 1990 and 1991. "There was never any doubt [illegible] his arm, and whatever. He knew how to throw from A to B. All we had to do was teach him how to throw to C."

Grbac impressed Bo Schembechler when he was thrown into the Notre Dame game as a freshman, and he almost passed the Wolverines to a win over the top-ranked Irish. After the job became all his as a sophomore, he led the Wolverines to three straight Big Ten titles and two Rose Bowls. During those seasons, Michigan averaged more than 34 points a game.

Maybe the most significant game was one of the five he lost—a 51–31 drubbing by Florida State in 1991. The defeat convinced the Michigan staff that the Wolverines had to get faster, and they changed their recruiting patterns.

Grbac's work ethic was legendary: He would practice pass patterns at the stadium with Howard and Derrick Alexander during long summer evenings. He never lost to Ohio State. In fact, the only time anyone saw him rattled was when a strong, quick Washington defense got to him repeatedly in the January 1992 game at Pasadena and held Michigan to its lowest point total of the year in a 34–14 beating.

Elvis was ready for the Rose Bowl rematch, and in his final college game he threw two touchdown passes in a 38–31 win over the Huskies. His best postseason performance had come in the January 1991 Gator Bowl against Mississippi, the first meeting between the two programs. Grbac threw four TD strikes, including 50- and 63-yard bombs to Howard and a 33-yarder to Alexander. The 715 yards of total offense that Michigan accumulated that day set a single-game school record.

Wheatley's Run for the Roses

Although Elvis Grbac tossed two touchdowns in the January 1993 Rose Bowl win over Washington, the game really belonged to Tyrone Wheatley. The Michigan tailback ran for three touchdowns and 235 yards against Washington in Michigan's 38–31 victory.

The triumph did not come easy. Even with Wheatley dashing for a 56-yard score in the second quarter, Michigan trailed 21–17 at the half. His 88-yard run from scrimmage, a Rose Bowl record, to open the third quarter didn't daunt Washington, either, and the Huskies moved in front once more, 31–24. But Wheatley's third long scoring run of the day, a 24-yard romp at the end of the third quarter, changed the game's momentum. The defense stopped the Huskies in the fourth quarter, and Grbac's 15-yard strike to Tony McGee won it.

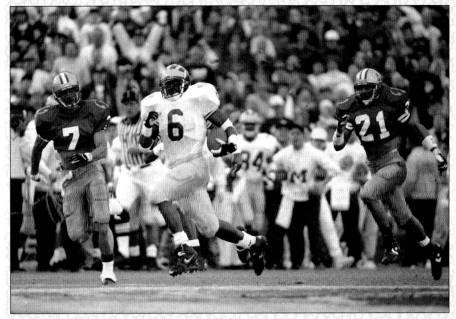

Wheatley blows through the Washington secondary during his 88-yard TD run.

Even the Wolverines and Buckeyes don't get as low-down and dirty as the fraternities and sororities that face each other in U-M's annual Mud Bowl.

Against Ohio State in 1995, Michigan's Tim Biakabutuka nearly tripled the yardage of Ohio State Heisman Trophy winner Eddie George, 313–105.

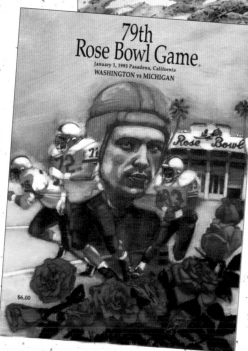

79th
Rose Bowl Game
January 1, 1993 Pasadena, California
WASHINGTON vs MICHIGAN

$6.00

The Rose Bowl not only hosted Michigan's thrilling 38–31 upset of Washington in January 1993, but it was the venue for Super Bowl XXVII later that month.

The Michigan Daily
SPORTSMONDAY
Michigan 31, Ohio State 23

Run Away

The Ohio State win is big – but not that big

Biakabutuka's 313 yards ruin Ohio State's title hopes

The Michigan Wolverines Mr. Potato Head would please U-M's running backs coach. The spud has learned to tuck in the ball and employ the stiff-arm!

The late Bob Ufer would certainly approve of this elaborate tailgate spread. Michigan tailgaters can party not just in parking lots but on the University Golf Course.

Rain and snow turned the 1995 Michigan-Purdue game into a slushy mess, as indicated by the final score: Michigan 5, Purdue 0.

Notre Dame is located so close to the Michigan border that the region surrounding it is called Michiana. Families in southwestern Michigan cities often have divided loyalties.

"Backyard Braggin Rights"
Michigan vs. Notre Dame

Mid-'90s Doldrums

Wisconsin was energized by new coach Barry Alvarez. Powerful Penn State entered the conference. Even Northwestern, the perennial doormat, rose to the top at one point. The Big Ten was shaken up top to bottom in the 1990s, and the end result was four straight three-loss seasons in the conference for the Wolverines (1993–96). It was the first time that had happened since the early 1960s. Right in the middle of all this was the unanticipated coaching change in 1995, when Lloyd Carr took over for Gary Moeller.

To add to the anxiety around the Michigan program, five of the 12 conference losses were in November, when championships are won and lost. All in all, the steam seemed to be leaking out of the Big House.

When Wisconsin finally broke through against Michigan for just the second time in 31 years with a 13–10 win in 1993, fans at Camp Randall Stadium tried to pour onto

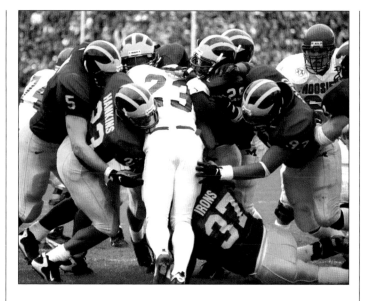

Seven Michigan defenders—close to a ton of humanity—consume an Indiana ball-carrier in 1996. From 1993 to '96, Indiana was one of just three Big Ten schools that did not celebrate a win over Michigan.

the field. The crush of humanity resulted in more than 70 injuries. Northwestern's 19–13 win in 1995 at Ann Arbor was its first over Michigan in 30 years. And when the Wildcats followed up with another victory in 1996, it was the first time they had beaten Michigan twice in a row since 1958–59.

The streak of winning seasons went on unabated, and there were still bowl games to play. But they were located in Tampa, San Diego, and San Antonio—not Michigan's accustomed New Year's Day haunt in Pasadena.

Bo Schembechler returned to Ann Arbor in 1993 after a brief stint as an executive with the Detroit Tigers. He sat in an office in the building that bore his name. Although he had no official status, he served as a consultant to Moeller and Carr. But the program he once had rescued seemed to have fallen back into the doldrums again.

Agony and Ecstasy

The most crushing defeat of this era was surely the 27–26 loss to Colorado on Michael Westbrook's end zone catch of a tipped, 64-yard desperation heave from Kordell Stewart as time ran out. It came in the third game of the 1994 season, and the Wolverines never seemed to gain traction afterward.

On the other hand, Michigan's first foray into August football furnished one of its most stirring finishes. In Lloyd Carr's first game as coach, in 1995, freshman quarterback Scott Dreisbach brought the Wolverines back from a 17–0 fourth-quarter deficit to beat Tiki Barber and Virginia 18–17. Mercury Hayes gathered in the winning score with one foot down in the end zone as time ran out. At the time, it was the largest margin Michigan had ever overcome.

The Carr Era Begins

Among Michigan's ten head coaches from 1901 through '07, Carr's .753 winning percentage ranked fifth, behind that of Fielding Yost, Fritz Crisler, Bo Schembechler, and Gary Moeller—in that order.

Lloyd Carr had been part of Michigan football as an assistant coach for 13 years when the job suddenly fell into his lap. Or hit him over the head, to be more precise. In a voice choking with emotion, he accepted the job as head coach before the 1995 season. He was furious at the dismissal of his longtime friend, Gary Moeller, and determined that the program would survive.

Carr had been a star quarterback at Northern Michigan. He coached as an assistant at Eastern Michigan, was hired by Moeller as an assistant at Illinois, and went with him to Ann Arbor in 1980. Carr developed a close relationship with Bo Schembechler, and when Lloyd was offered a job as an assistant at Notre Dame, Bo was against it. "You're a

Michigan man," he said with words more prophetic than he knew.

Carr was a more soothing presence than either Bo or Moe. Though tough when he had to be, he favored a more encouraging approach, leaving the discipline and tough talk to his assistants. He was given the title "interim," but as his first season wore on it became apparent that the program was in good hands. Michigan started 5–0 and was ranked sixth in the country before losing to a formidable Northwestern team. The job was made permanent a month later.

Carr had taken over under terrible circumstances and restored the program to equilibrium. But in this case, equilibrium meant two more four-loss seasons (9–4 in 1995 and 8–4 in '96). Carr admitted later that he had heard the grumbling in the media and among the alumni. The Michigan brass wasn't about to push the eject button, but there was reason for apprehension.

The quarterback position was unstable. Scott Dreisbach was inconsistent and Brian Griese was suspended from the team before the 1996 season after an altercation at an Ann Arbor bar. Big Ten offenses had opened up a lot since Bo's heyday, but even allowing for that the Michigan defense was not what it once was. In Moeller's last year, it had given up 268 points, the worst in Michigan history. The defense improved slightly in 1995, but it was still a shaky proposition.

When the 1997 season began, it appeared that Michigan was on the edge. Experts no longer considered U-M to be among the nation's elite. There was work to be done.

Record-Breaking Backs

Although Michigan finally committed itself to a full-bore passing attack, the line of prime running backs continued undiminished after 1990. From Tyrone Wheatley to Mike Hart, Michigan's backs were as reliable as another 100,000 crowd in the Big House.

Wheatley saved his best performances for the bowls. In four postseason games, he rushed for seven touchdowns and 507 yards, including three runs of more than 50 yards. His Rose Bowl MVP performance of 1993 was followed by another trophy-winning job against North Carolina State in the next year's Hall of Fame Bowl. In the 42–7 rout, he scored his 35th career rushing TD, breaking Rick Leach's school record. Most observers felt his midseason shoulder injury, during which the Wolverines lost twice after late fumbles, kept Michigan from a sixth straight Big Ten title.

Tshimanga "Tim" Biakabutuka, a rare recruit from Zaire by way of Quebec, was at his most explosive during the 1995 season. He rushed for a Michigan-record 1,818 yards, including a 313-yard effort against Ohio State. "I didn't see holes that big even in high school," he said after that game. "Bazooka" would have been a perfect nickname for Biaka-

butuka, but sportswriters called him "Touchdown Tim."

Anthony Thomas was the most consistent running back in Michigan history. Nicknamed the "A Train," the Louisiana native finished with 4,472 yards, 55 rushing TDs, and 22 100-yard rushing games—all of which broke school records. Durable and fast, Thomas could pound inside all game long and then break loose from lunging linebackers.

While Thomas earned second-team All-America honors, Chris Perry was a first-teamer in 2003, when he also became the first Michigan player to win the Doak Walker Award as the country's top running back. His performance against Michigan State, in which he lugged the ball a school-record 51 times for 219 yards, was one of the most courageous efforts in school history. Almost single-handedly, he kept the ball out of Spartan hands late in the game in a tough 27–20 win.

Largely overlooked because of his 5'9" frame, and the fact that he played for a small high school, Hart answered all doubts as a freshman and never looked back. A four-year starter with the Wolverines, Hart graduated after the 2007 season as Michigan's career rushing leader with 5,040 yards, which ranked fourth in Big Ten history.

Running back Chris Perry finished fourth in Heisman Trophy voting in 2003 after he ran—and sometimes flew—for 1,674 yards and 18 touchdowns.

Running back Mike Hart amassed more 100-yard rushing games (28) and more 200 yard rushing performances (five) than any other player in Michigan history.

12–0 and National Champs!

Something had changed. You could sense it from the moment the team took the field in the 1997 opener against Colorado. The Buffaloes were a dangerous team, coming off two straight 10–2 seasons under their young, offensive-minded coach, Rick Neuheisel.

The Michigan defense took them apart. Pressuring and sacking the quarterback over and over again, the Wolverines overwhelmed Colorado 27–3. The following week, they did the same to Baylor in a 38–3 romp.

This was the sort of defensive intensity Michigan fans hadn't seen in years. It was constantly attacking, and the rush was liable to come from any direction at any time.

Charles Woodson's spectacular one-handed interception helped Michigan beat MSU 23–7 in 1997, which improved the Wolverines' record to 7–0.

You could see the confidence growing on every series of downs. The defensive unit exchanged quick looks that said: "They can't stop us."

Young defensive coordinator Jim Herrmann had designed this scheme, and his players bought into it completely. Over the course of the season, they allowed fewer than ten points a game.

The pattern actually had been set in the last regular-season game of 1996, a major upset of unbeaten,

Michigan scored only once in the first half of the 1998 Rose Bowl—on this 56-yard pass play from Brian Griese to Tai Streets. The Wolverines beat Washington State 21–16.

second-ranked Ohio State. Brian Griese, coming off the bench, threw a second-half touchdown pass to Tai Streets, and the defense shut down OSU's big offense in a 13–9 victory. Even during a loss in the Outback Bowl to Alabama, Michigan allowed just 17 points. The defense had stopped two major teams and was eager to be tested again.

Anchored by linebacker Sam Sword, end Glen Steele, and, most of all, cornerback Charles Woodson, it was a defense that captured the imagination of Michigan fans. Even a scare against Iowa in week six, when Michigan trailed by two touchdowns at the half, didn't shake their confidence. A late rally pulled it out, 28–24. When the Wolverines stormed into Happy Valley and mauled unbeaten Penn State 34–8, hundreds of students marched

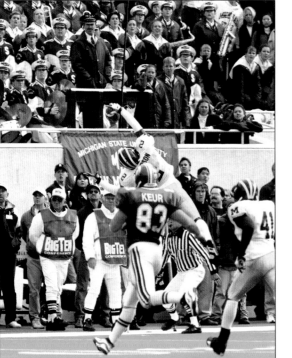

to university president Lee Bollinger's house to rejoice and were invited inside by the bemused academic.

But the season came down, as it always did, to Ohio State. Michigan had taken a possible national title away from the Buckeyes the previous year, and everyone knew that the fourth-ranked OSU team was desperate to return the favor. The crowd of 106,982 at the Big House was another record, and fans arrived with the usual mixture of elation and dread.

But Woodson made sure of a happy ending. With Michigan leading 7–0, he gathered in a punt at his own 22, eluded one tackler, made a stagger step to get past another, and then ran down the left sideline behind a wall of blockers. You could see the play develop from every part of the stadium, and by the time Woodson reached midfield,

A Heisman for Woodson

The stats don't even begin to tell the story. They never do when it comes to a defensive player. Yes, Charles Woodson's eight interceptions ranked second nationally. His big picks in the Ohio State and Rose Bowl games helped decide them. His one-handed interception along the sideline against Michigan State became an iconic image of the magical 1997 season.

All those plays contributed to his Heisman Trophy, the first ever given to a predominantly defensive player. But what the stats don't show is how he shut down half the field from opposing passers. Almost no one dared to throw in his direction. Moreover, his 238 yards as a pass receiver added another dimension to the offense. Tellingly, as Brian Griese led Michigan to its final clinching Rose Bowl drive, it was Woodson to whom he turned on two critical third-and-long situations to keep it going. He was the single most dominant figure on the field every time he walked onto it in 1997.

totally in the clear, the place was going berserk. OSU made it close, but Woodson intercepted a pass in the end zone and the Wolverines prevailed 20–14. The supposedly blasé Michigan students rushed the field in a display of emotion that hadn't been seen in Ann Arbor in years.

Then it was on to the Rose Bowl and a date with Washington State for the national title. Griese threw three touchdown strikes (two to Streets), but the defense had its hands full with the wide-open Cougars aerial attack.

With Michigan clinging to a 21–16 lead, Griese engineered a masterful drive, overcoming four third downs, to leave WSU with just 29 seconds and no timeouts left when it got the ball back. As his father, legendary Miami Dolphins quarterback Bob Griese, watched tearfully from the broadcast booth, the MVP Award was presented to the Wolverines' quarterback.

Michigan was deprived of a clear-cut title when the coaches poll switched to Nebraska, marking the only time in history that a No. 1 team had won its bowl game and slipped in the rankings. But the Wolverines took the AP verdict, and that was plenty good enough.

His father, Bob Griese, quarterbacked the Miami Dolphins to a perfect season in 1972, and Brian did the same for Michigan in 1997. Later, they coauthored a book entitled Undefeated.

After OSU receiver David Boston dissed Charles Woodson before their 1997 encounter, Woodson responded with a brilliant game. He returned a punt for a touchdown and picked off a Buckeyes pass in the Wolverines' end zone.

After returning from Christmas break, Michigan students enjoyed this commemorative Rose Bowl section in *The Michigan Daily*.

Charles Woodson displays the Heisman Trophy, which he won by a comfortable margin in 1997 over Tennessee's Peyton Manning.

In 1998, for the last time, more than 100,000 fans attended a Rose Bowl game. The stadium was subsequently modified, with thousands of seats removed.

"Men, you have left a lasting legacy," coach Lloyd Carr told his players in the Rose Bowl locker room. "You have just won the national championship!"

Sports Illustrated began publishing commemorative editions of NCAA football champions in the early 1990s. With millions of Michigan fans across the country, SI had no trouble selling copies of this special issue.

The Bigger House

An annoying thing happened during the course of the 1997 championship season. The University of Tennessee expanded its stadium, and Michigan—despite not drawing fewer than 106,000 fans to the Big House that season—fell to second in average attendance for the first time in 24 years. It was a challenge that had to be addressed.

So in 1998, Michigan Stadium's capacity was increased for the sixth time. The renovations raised the number of "official" seats to 107,501, but the game against Michigan State attracted 111,238 to set an NCAA record.

Network television announcer Keith Jackson is credited with being the first to refer to the stadium as the "Big House." The name caught on immediately. Knowing they are part of "the largest crowd to watch a football game in America today," as the public address announcer customarily intones in the fourth quarter, makes Michigan fans proud. Getting knocked from that perch was almost as dis-

Less-Artificial Turf

The turf at the Big House is a story in itself. The artificial surface, installed in 1969, was replaced by the real stuff in 1991. But reality had its limits.

It was determined by the Board of Regents that a new surface called Field-Turf was superior in terms of maintenance cost, drainage, and player safety. So before the 2003 season, in it went. The surface consists primarily of crushed rubber, and much of the material came through a donation from the Ford Motor Company.

The renovations also included tripling the size of the home locker room. For the first time, all Michigan players could dress right at the stadium. The safer turf and the more comfortable accommodations gave recruits two more reasons to say yes to Michigan.

tressing as not going to a January bowl. So the expansion was approved almost by popular demand. A halo placed around the stadium exterior proved to be less popular and was eventually removed.

Attendance figures of more than 111,000, and on one occasion more than 112,000, have become commonplace for the biggest games. Other stadiums now exceed the six-figure capacity level, a figure that was Michigan's alone in 1956. But the Big House retains its edge.

What makes the attendance story even more amazing is that virtually every Michigan home game has been on television since cable arrived in the 1980s. The wisdom of Don Canham's strategy to sell a total experience rather than a game has never been clearer.

Michigan Stadium continues to inspire awe from anyone entering it for the first time—or the thousandth. Since 1927, the stadium has played host to more than 40 million fans.

In Michigan, only seven cities have populations that exceed this one stadium's capacity: Detroit, Grand Rapids, Warren, Sterling Heights, Flint, Lansing, and Ann Arbor.

Parade of Quarterbacks

Chad Henne's passing yards dropped each of his four seasons (he was injured as a senior). However, his 9,715 career yards set a Michigan record, and his 87 touchdown passes ranked second in Big Ten history.

Despite the succession of pro style, drop back passers that started for Michigan after 1990, none was a first round selection in the NFL Draft. In fact, none of them even earned All-America honors. Over the same time span, however, four Michigan wide receivers were taken in the first round. Maybe they were throwing the ball to themselves.

It's understandable why these quarterbacks dropped in the draft. At a time when the NFL began to emphasize height and mobility, these Wolverines were notoriously slow afoot.

Not that it mattered much to Tom Brady. During his two seasons as the starter, in 1998–99, he led the Wolverines to a 20–5 record and bowl wins over Arkansas and Alabama. He set records for pass completions in a season in 1998, yet he still managed to fly under the radar. Part of that was because he rarely was used in his first two seasons and had to share playing time with the heir apparent, Drew Henson, as a senior. Brady fell all the way to the sixth round in the NFL Draft, where the New England Patriots—to their everlasting joy—found him.

Henson was one of the most heralded athletes ever to show up in Ann Arbor. He was the top prospect in the state and a star in baseball as well as football. But there was the rub. After one year as a starter, he chose to take a big money offer from New York Yankees owner (and Ohio State alumnus) George Steinbrenner.

Lloyd Carr will never say who his favorite player was, but if asked about the most courageous, he will unhesitatingly say John Navarre. Navarre was rushed in as a starter far ahead of the timetable because of the abrupt departure of Henson. He struggled at the outset and came under heavy criticism from fans and media. But he never wavered, and when he graduated after the 2003 season, he held most Michigan passing marks and a conference title.

Chad Henne was also a quarterback before his time, leading the team as a freshman in 2004 because of a preseason injury to the designated starter. Michigan went to two Rose Bowls in his first three years, and he surpassed most of Navarre's career records.

The highest choice by the NFL Draft during this period was, in fact, Todd Collins. He was chosen in the second round by Buffalo in 1995 after two straight four-loss seasons and never being named to the All-Big Ten team. But that's the NFL for you.

John Navarre led Michigan to the Big Ten title in 2003. He threw for 3,331 yards that year, making him up through Chad Henne's senior season the only U-M quarterback to eclipse 3,000 yards.

Bowl Game Three-Peat

Orlando and Miami are not bad consolation prizes when it comes to bowl games. Michigan took full advantage of its three bowl trips to Florida following the 1998 to 2000 seasons to come away with three victories—a welcome reversal from its previous bowl history.

After two early losses in 1998, to Notre Dame and Syracuse, the Wolverines ripped off eight wins in a row. Their loss to Ohio State put them in a three-way first-place tie with the Buckeyes and Wisconsin. Since Wisconsin (whom Michigan had defeated) had not been to Pasadena as recently as U-M or Ohio State, the Badgers got to go.

Michigan went to the Citrus Bowl in Orlando to play Arkansas. Tom Brady threw for 209 yards, Tai Streets amassed 129 yards in reception yardage, and Anthony Thomas ran for 132 yards in a 45–31 win. But the numbers are deceiving. Michigan actually squandered a halftime lead and trailed 31–24 in the fourth quarter before three straight touchdowns put the Razorbacks away.

The 1999 campaign was almost a duplicate, with Michigan again handling conference champion Wisconsin, 21–16. But after Michigan's painful midseason losses to Michigan State and Illinois, the Badgers returned to Pasadena and Michigan headed to the Orange Bowl to play fifth-ranked Alabama. The Wolverines celebrated their first football game of the 21st century with a thrilling 35–34 overtime win.

In 2000, Drew Henson's one season as a starter, Michigan lost three games by a total of seven points, including a 54–51 defeat by Northwestern, one of the strangest games in Michigan history. With Michigan trying to run out the clock, Thomas fumbled. That allowed the Wildcats to stage a wild last-second comeback. Purdue got the Roses, while Michigan settled for a 31–28 Citrus win over Auburn. Henson completed 15 of 20 for 294 yards in his last game as a Wolverine.

Michigan place-kicker Jay Feely rumbles through the Wisconsin defense on a fake field goal in their 1998 contest. U-M won 27–10, but the Badgers went to the Rose Bowl.

Brady's Super Bowl

If the pro scouts had been paying attention, they would have seen Tom Brady's performance in the 2000 Orange Bowl as a glimpse of things to come. It was one of the great Michigan passing shows of all time, with Brady twice bringing the team back from 14-point deficits. He ended up with 369 yards passing against an Alabama defense that had completely shut down Michigan's running game.

Tom Brady (left) wtih Jason Kapner

Brady hit wide receiver David Terrell three times for touchdowns before Anthony Thomas finally banged over from three yards out to tie it, 28–28. In overtime, tight end Shawn Thompson caught Brady's fourth TD strike. Alabama also scored on its possession, but when the extra-point attempt sailed wide Michigan celebrated a 35–34 victory.

Rifle-armed quarterback Drew Henson led Michigan to a 38–26 win over Ohio State in 2000. Henson went on to play briefly in both the NFL and the major leagues.

21st Century Classics

The Little Brown Jug was in distinct peril of becoming a Little Brown Dud. Once Michigan's nemesis, Minnesota had managed to defeat the Wolverines just twice from 1968 through 2002, while losing 31 times. But this lopsided rivalry provided the greatest comeback in Wolverines history in the 2003 game at Minneapolis.

The Gophers had undergone a resurgence under coach Glen Mason, and when the teams met they were ranked No. 17, three spots ahead of Michigan. The Wolverines' defense had been punctured for 30 points or more in losses to Oregon and Iowa, and it appeared that Minnesota was going to surpass that mark.

The Gophers' running attack was unstoppable, piling up 424 yards—a record for a Michigan opponent. By the end of the third quarter, it was a 28–7 rout. But with John Navarre operating from the shotgun, Michigan scored a quick touchdown, and then a returned interception made it 28–21. Minnesota came right back with a 52-yard TD run. The Wolverines brushed it aside, and Navarre hit Braylon Edwards on a 52-yard touchdown strike. Minnesota then gave up a long punt return by Steve Breaston and a ten-yard run by Chris Perry and suddenly it was a 35–35 tie. With 47 seconds to go, a 33-yard Garrett Rivas field goal won it. Incredibly, the Wolverines had scored 31 points in the fourth quarter. The comeback helped them earn a Big Ten title and a trip to Pasadena.

Receiver Mario Manningham sucks in a touchdown pass with no time left on the clock in Michigan's 27–25 win over Penn State in 2005. Through 2007, Michigan had beaten the Lions nine times in a row.

The 2005 Penn State game may not have been quite as wild, but in terms of last-second suspense it may have been the tops. The Lions arrived undefeated and ready to wipe out the memory of a long dry spell against Michigan. Instead, Chad Henne hit Mario Manningham in the back of the end zone from ten yards out with no time left for a 27–25 win. Michigan had marched down the field with under a minute left after a Penn State go-ahead touchdown. Only because Lloyd Carr convinced the officials to put two seconds back on the clock on a disputed timeout call was there any time left at all. In a season in which Michigan lost three games when it could not hold a fourth-quarter lead, this was the most dramatic of turnabouts.

In 2002 Penn State fell victim to last-second Wolverine theatrics. Navarre led Michigan down the field in the fourth quarter to force overtime, in which U-M prevailed 27–24. In Michigan's home opener that season, Philip Brabbs split the uprights with a 44-yard field goal as time expired to defeat Washington 31–29. These dramatic victories helped offset several nightmarish endings—from Texas's field goal in the 2005 Rose Bowl to the 2007 debacle against Appalachian State.

Coach Lloyd Carr congratulates Philip Brabbs after his game-ending field goal against Washington in 2002—his first for Michigan. If it weren't for a 15-yard penalty on the previous play, Brabbs's 44-yard attempt would have been 59 yards.

Game Day in Ann Arbor

Six to eight Saturdays each fall, Ann Arbor swells in size and Michigan Stadium becomes the seventh most populous "city" in the state. The cognoscenti know they better get on the road early because freeways and surface streets will be jammed three hours before kickoff. It also pays to have a cordial relationship with a parking lot operator—or else hoof it for a mile or so from the garages downtown.

> "Grown men cry when they hear their son's name announced playing for Michigan. I owed it to them to always get it right."
>
> **Howard King, former public address announcer**

The great appeal is the timelessness of football in Ann Arbor. The quintessential college town and the most successful college football program make an unbeatable combination.

Some tailgates have been going on for 30 years or more. Newlyweds who began gathering with friends now reminisce as their grandchildren toss a Frisbee across the parking lots. Some even bring their own TV dish hookup to keep up with the pregame shows on ESPN.

The classic approach is the walk across The Quad and then down State Street. The crowd swells as you move along—past parties at a few frat houses and trailers where radio stations are doing remote game day broadcasts. Many stop in for French toast at Angelo's (although they better get there extra early for that) or a stick-to-the-ribs sandwich at Zingerman's—or perhaps even a Blimpy Burger from Krazy Jim's.

The human tide swells as it crosses Packard and then turns right onto Hoover Street. If you timed this right, you will near Revelli Hall just as the marching band comes pouring out of its headquarters. It forms in the middle of the street and, for the first of a few dozen times that day, blasts "The Victors." Some fans try to fall in behind the band and turn left with it onto Greene Street for the final approach to the Big House.

How is it possible to spend a better autumn Saturday?

Tailgaters arrive hours early for Michigan games—out of choice and necessity. The amount of traffic flowing into Ann Arbor just before each game is enormous.

55th Annual
CapitalOne
FLORIDA CITRUS BOWL
Auburn vs. Michigan
Monday • 1 P.M. • January 1, 2001 • Orlando, Florida

In the 2001 Citrus Bowl, Michigan racked up 456 yards against the SEC's top defense. Drew Henson threw for 294 yards and Anthony Thomas ran for 182 as Michigan beat Auburn 31–28.

It happens at least six times a year, but it never fails to excite: The Big House erupts in jubilation when the Wolverines sky to touch the M Club banner while the band plays "The Victors."

This complete set of 2002 tickets reminded fans of the joys of attending a Michigan football game.

MICHIGAN GAME DAY TRADITIONS

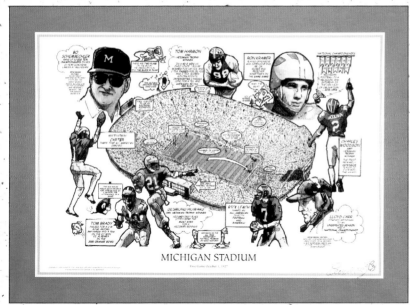

This illustration by Leonard D. Fritz includes arrows pointing to the spots of memorable plays, such as Desmond Howard's touchdown catch against Notre Dame in 1991.

Michigan cheerleaders may be most distinguishable by their maize and blue pom-poms and their perpetual cries of "Let's go, Blue!"

The first day of the 21st century turned out great. The Y2K computer crisis was averted, and Tom Brady led Michigan to an OT Orange Bowl victory over Alabama.

Thousands of Michigan Wolverines products are available online, from barbecues and birdfeeders to this commemorative stein.

Crushing the Buckeyes

Ohio State hired John Cooper as its coach because he was identified as the man most likely to beat Michigan. That was a good theory, based on how Cooper's Arizona State had handled the Wolverines in the 1987 Rose Bowl. In practice, though, it fell somewhat short.

In the 13 years Cooper coached the Buckeyes, from 1988 to 2000, he went 2–10–1 against Michigan. In four of those losses, OSU was the higher ranked team. Two years in a row, they came into the Michigan game undefeated, only to be felled by rather ordinary U-M squads.

It was U-M's most sustained period of dominance over the Buckeyes in 50 years. From 1938 to 1951, Michigan had run up a 10–2–2 mark against OSU, which resulted in Woody Hayes going to Columbus to remedy matters.

Cooper became a likely candidate for the moving van in his first four years, losing each game against Michigan. Two of those losses came in the last minute and a half, one on a J. D. Carlson field goal as time ran out in 1990. The loss kept OSU from the Rose Bowl. Amid rumors that he was a goner, Cooper managed to eke out a 13–13 tie against an unbeaten Michigan team in 1992, and then got a satisfying first win, 22–6, in 1994.

But the frustration mounted in 1995 when Tim Biakabutuka ran wild, rushing for 313 yards and keying a huge 31–23 upset of unbeaten OSU. Then it happened again the following year. Brian Griese came off the bench to fire a touchdown pass to Tai Streets, and the Michigan defense quelled the Buckeyes 13–9. That loss probably cost the Buckeyes the national championship since they went on to beat undefeated Arizona State in the Rose Bowl.

Thirsting for payback in 1997, the Buckeyes instead were thwarted by Charles Woodson's heroics in Michigan's 20–14 win. Another Buckeyes loss in 1999 during a 6–6 season, and a final 38–26 bashing in 2000 at the hands of Drew Henson, who threw for 303 yards, made it curtains for Cooper. "I can't hide behind it," he said afterward. "My record is just awful."

But OSU had Jim Tressel waiting in the wings, and he righted the ship quicker than anyone since Woody. In his very first shot at the Wolverines, in 2001, his four-loss team took Michigan out of the Rose Bowl in a convincing 26–20 win. The next year, led by tailback Maurice Clarett, an unbeaten OSU team finally cleared the hurdle, stopping Michigan 14–9 on the way to a national title.

In the 2003 centennial game, Lloyd Carr finally got in his licks against Tressel. The 35–21 Michigan win, behind the passing of John Navarre and the running of Chris Perry, took OSU right out of the chance for a repeat BCS title game and sent the Wolverines to the Rose Bowl for the first time in six years.

Over the next two seasons, however, quarterback Troy Smith ran and passed circles around the Wolverines. In 2004 security at Ohio Stadium insisted on searching the Michigan players for weapons before allowing them inside. There was no reciprocal pettiness in 2005, and Smith brought OSU down the field in Ann Arbor for two touchdowns in the last few minutes for a stressful 25–21 win.

That set the stage for 2006, when two undefeated powerhouses would collide, just as in the good old days with Bo and Woody.

Michigan's swarming defense kept Ohio State in check in 1990. The Wolverines prevailed 16–13 on J. D. Carlson's 37-yard field goal as time expired.

Florida Vacations

The departure of Drew Henson before his time was a shock to the Wolverines' system. The orderly progression of starting quarterbacks was interrupted, and John Navarre had to be rushed into the breach. Although he led Michigan to an 18–7 record in his first two seasons as a full-time starter, it was often a struggle.

The 2001 team sometimes sputtered on offense, and its 320 points were the fewest scored by a Michigan team in five years. Worsening matters, the defense could not bail them out, giving up double digits in 11 of 12 games. Michigan walloped 2001 Big Ten champion Illinois 45–20 but lost close games at Washington and Michigan State. Though Michigan still had a shot at the Rose Bowl, OSU pressure forced Navarre into repeated mistakes in a 26–20 Buckeyes victory. The final defeat sent the Wolverines back to the Citrus Bowl, where they ran into a Tennessee team that had just been waiting for a shot at them.

Volunteers fans were still aggrieved that Charles Woodson had been chosen for the Heisman in 1997 over their own Peyton Manning, who had remained in school for his senior year partially to get his hands on that trophy. When Tennessee got the chance, it made the most of it. The 45–17 beating was the worst ever for Michigan in a bowl game. Casey Clausen dented the Wolverines for 393 yards passing and five touchdowns, two by foot. He was still throwing with a 38–10 fourth-quarter lead.

It was pretty much more of the same in 2002. Tight losses to Notre Dame and Ohio State were punctuated by an absolute wipeout by Iowa, 34–9, at the Big House. The end result was another bowl trip to Florida, where the Wolverines met the University of Florida in the Outback Bowl. This time, Michigan met the challenge.

Chris Perry ran for four touchdowns and Navarre passed for a key score to Ronald Bellamy just before the half. The Wolverines' defense kept constant pressure on quarterback Rex Grossman, recovered two fumbles, and had enough to hold off a late charge, 38–30. It was a satisfactory finish. But the measure at Michigan is always the Rose Bowl, and Michigan hadn't been back there since the 1997 championship season. Patience was running thin.

Tennessee receiver Dante Stallworth (who would team with Tom Brady in New England) burns Jeremy LeSueur in the 2002 Citrus Bowl. The Volunteers crushed the Wolverines 45–17— Michigan's largest margin of defeat since the 1968 Ohio State game.

Running back B. J. Askew flies sideways into the Wisconsin end zone in 2002. After beating the Badgers 21–14, Michigan lost its next game, against Ohio State, before defeating Florida in the Outback Bowl.

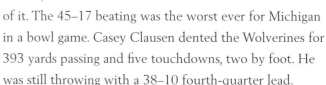

Sticky-Finger Receivers

Great running teams usually have great defenses because they can dominate time of possession. But it doesn't hurt to have some guys who can go and get the bomb, too.

Since Anthony Carter and Desmond Howard set the standard, Michigan had drawn some of the top wideouts in America. A steady progression of stellar receivers—Derrick Alexander, Amani Toomer, David Terrell, Marquise Walker, Braylon Edwards, Mario Manningham—has given quarterbacks lots of chances to move the chains.

Alexander was Howard's running mate for a season, then broke out in spectacular fashion in 1992 as a receiver and punt returner. He was the first Wolverine to return punts for touchdowns in consecutive games, and his 90-yard touchdown reception against Illinois in 1993 was the longest in team history.

Terrell was the first Michigan receiver to record two 1,000-yard seasons (1999–2000), and his 1,130 yards in the latter year was a school record. The mark lasted just one year, though, as Walker eclipsed it by 13 yards in 2001. Although often overlooked on the list of great receivers, Walker set records that year with six 100-yard games, two games with 15 receptions, and 86 catches for the season.

Tai Streets was playing in a more run-oriented offense in 1996–98, but his two long touchdown catches helped win the January 1998 Rose Bowl. He still ranks in Michigan's career top ten in catches, yards, and touchdowns.

In addition to the wideouts, Michigan also produced two all-conference tight ends in this era with Jerame Tuman and Bennie Joppru. Tuman, a favorite target of Brian Griese in 1997, was instrumental in sustaining the ball-control offense that year. Joppru teamed with John Navarre to set a Michigan record with 53 receptions by a tight end in 2002.

Michigan wideout Marquise Walker makes an insane touchdown catch against Iowa in 2001. Walker was named an All-American that year after breaking school records for receptions (86) and receiving yards (1,143).

Braylon's No. 1

Braylon Edwards

If ever a Michigan player was born to be No. 1, it was Braylon Edwards. His father, Stan Edwards, was a starting running back for Michigan in the early 1980s, and Braylon was sometimes taken to visit Bo as an infant. As Braylon got older, he vowed to play wide receiver and to wear the fabled No. 1. That was Anthony Carter's number, and it had been given to a only small number of worthy receivers, including Greg McMurtry and David Terrell.

Edwards ended up shattering most of their records. After his final season in 2004, he held the Michigan marks for receptions with 252, total yardage with 3,541, most games of 100 yards with 17, and TD catches with 39, which was also a Big Ten record. He became one of the few receivers in NCAA history to gain more than 1,000 yards in three straight years.

Back to Pasadena

Chris Perry leaps over the Illinois defense and into the end zone during Michigan's 56–14 rout in 2003. The Wolverines scored 460 points that season, most by a U-M team since 1905.

Some Big Ten programs would dance with joy at a Rose Bowl every five years. But at Michigan, five years represented the longest absence from Pasadena since 1964.

Almost on schedule, however, the Wolverines came back in 2003, in John Navarre's senior year. The quarterback still had his critics, but there was no denying that a retooled Michigan offense was potent once again. With Braylon Edwards, Jason Avant, and Steve Breaston as wide receivers and Chris Perry at tailback, Michigan ran up 460 points, a new high in the modern era.

After the first three games, they had outscored opponents 133–10, and that included a 38–0 whomping of Notre Dame. But then a familiar bugaboo popped up. The Wolverines had developed a habit of stumbling in their first road game of the year. They had done it four times in the previous five years, and now Oregon sprung the trap, knocking them off 31–27 at Eugene. Iowa also took them out at Iowa City, 30–27, and only a semi-miraculous fourth quarter comeback held off Minnesota on the road, 38–35.

But after those bumps, Navarre put the pedal to the metal and the Wolverines cruised through their final five games without a hitch. Needing a win against Ohio State in the finale, Michigan used all its weapons in the 35–21 win. Navarre connected with Edwards for two touchdowns, Perry scored two more, and Breaston scored on a gadget play—running a quarterback option. "We've tasted greatness, but we never really got it," said Perry. "I wanted to be remembered."

Back in Pasadena, however, Michigan ran into a buzz saw against top-ranked (at least, in the AP poll) Southern California. It could not contain Matt Leinart's passing attack, as he threw three touchdown passes and caught one himself from wideout Mike Williams. Michigan went down decisively, 28–14.

USC's LenDale White sneaks into the end zone in the 2004 Rose Bowl. The Trojans were not invited to the National Championship Game, but after their 28–14 win over Michigan, the AP voted them No. 1.

The 2004 season presented a new set of challenges. Edwards, the top receiver in college football, was back. But junior quarterback Matt Gutierrez, who had been groomed to take over for Navarre, went down with a shoulder injury during the preseason. Next on the depth chart was true freshman Chad Henne. Suddenly Michigan was right back where it had been when Navarre had to be rushed in for Drew Henson in 2001.

Playing with poise beyond his years, though, Henne grabbed hold of the offense and made it work, aided by a fellow freshman, running back Mike Hart. A conservative game plan held Henne back at South Bend—never an easy place to play under the best of conditions—and Notre Dame took care of business, 28–20.

After that, however, Henne sailed through the conference schedule. There were close calls against Purdue and Minnesota, but otherwise Michigan never scored fewer than three touchdowns. By the time the Wolverines reached the Ohio State game, the Big Ten title and the trip to Pasadena were already nailed down.

Still, that was no balm for what Troy Smith and the Buckeyes did, pounding Michigan rather easily, 37–21. It was the most points the Buckeyes had run up against UM since the 50-point affair in 1968. Defensive coordinator Jim Herrmann had been hailed as a hero after his scheme won a national title in 1997. But in the years since then, his defenses had given up an average of 244 points. The OSU game, with Smith's elusiveness in avoiding an ineffective rush, seemed to underscore the problem. What happened in Pasadena proved to be the clincher.

Defensive backs Ernest Shazor (left) and Marlin Jackson agonize over the Longhorns' successful field goal that ended the dramatic 2005 Rose Bowl.

Hooked by the Horns

If Troy Smith gave Michigan's defense fits in 2004, Texas quarterback Vince Young had players banging their fists in the air in frustration. On New Year's Day, 2005, in one of the greatest Rose Bowls ever played, Young ran for 192 yards, passed for 180, and scored four touchdowns. Then as time ran out, Dusty Mangum's wobbly field goal attempt made it through the uprights in a 38–37 Texas triumph.

Chad Henne, the first true freshman quarterback ever to start a Rose Bowl, was almost a match for Young all the way. He tied a Rose Bowl record with four TD passes, three of them to Edwards, while Steve Breaston's 315 all-purpose yards kept the Wolverines in great field position. In the end, however, the defense could not hold on, and the 75 points allowed in the final two games were a cause for alarm.

U-M fans celebrate their team's 35–21 victory over Ohio State at the Big House in 2003. For the first time in six years, Michigan was going to the Rose Bowl.

Real wolverines do not exist in the wild in Michigan, but this sculpture of the tenacious critter lurks among the trees near the stadium entrance.

This 2003 ticket set includes rivalry images for every featured team—except the University of Houston, which Michigan had faced (and routed) only in 1992 and '93.

In September 2006, General Mills honored Michigan (along with Georgia and Notre Dame) with special packaging. Perhaps General Mills anticipated U-M's 11–0 start!

REMEMBERING BO
TRIBUTES, TEARS AND TESTIMONIES FOR THE FACE OF MICHIGAN FOOTBALL
SPECIAL SECTION

Bond: ★★★★
ARTS, 5A

The Michigan Daily

OHIO STATE 42, MICHIGAN 39

THE ONE THAT GOT AWAY

But title game still in reach

No. 2 rank in BCS gives 'M' hope

Despite losing their 2006 game against Ohio State, Michigan had a chance for a rematch in the National Championship Game. However, Florida got to go after edging out U-M in the BCS rankings.

OKLAHOMA — THE BCS RACE FOR THE — USC
NATIONAL CHAMPIONSHIP
PLUS LSU'S CHANCES

Sports Illustrated

MICHIGAN
GETS IT DONE
BY AUSTIN MURPHY

EXCLUSIVE INTERVIEW
TOKYO CALLING: KAZUO MATSUI
NBA: WILL THE WEST RULE FOREVER?

Sports Illustrated gave the 2003 Michigan-Ohio State game top coverage. The Buckeyes, who entered the game at 10–1, lost, and Michigan went to the Rose Bowl.

Michigan fans pay tribute to Bo Schembechler in an emotional nighttime vigil. Bo died on November 17, 2006, just hours after delivering a pep talk for the Michigan-Ohio State game.

In 2003, an NCAA-record 112,118 fans watched Michigan win its 100th meeting against Ohio State, 35–21.

MICHIGAN O OHIO STATE
100th
GAME
ANN ARBOR
MICHIGAN
SATURDAY NOVEMBER 23 · TWO THOUSAND AND THREE

The Intrastate War

It seemed that George Perles had returned Michigan State football to state supremacy with his 1987 conference title and Rose Bowl win. But Michigan bounced right back, beating the Spartans in 12 of the next 17 games against Perles and three successors. Every State win seemed to take place under extraordinary circumstances, and its losses were crushing.

The 1990 game was typical. Michigan was ranked first in the nation and was a 11-point favorite. But State drove the field four times on the Wolverines and held a 28–21 lead in the closing minutes. With seconds remaining, Elvis Grbac hit Derrick Alexander for a touchdown. Gary Moeller passed up the tie and decided to go for the two-point conversion. Desmond Howard, after being illegally grabbed by Eddie Brown, caught the pass in the end zone and then dropped it when he hit the turf. Either a penalty or a two-point conversion could have been called, but instead it was ruled an incomplete pass. The Spartans won 28–27. Only later in the week did the Big Ten admit that the call was wrong and that interference should have given Michigan another shot. Too late.

More controversy erupted in 2001, when a desperate State drive to the goal seemed to run out of time with Michigan ahead by four. Somehow, however, the clock at Spartan Stadium stopped running when it hit 0:01. With one more play granted to them, the Spartans got into the end zone to topple the Wolverines 26–24.

> ## "I'm just sick."
>
> ### Michigan State coach John L. Smith after Michigan's improbable comeback in 2004

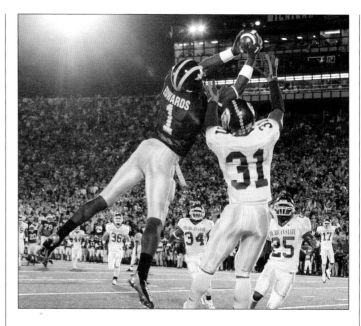

Braylon Edwards snatches a touchdown pass against Michigan State during their amazing comeback in 2004. The Wolverines won in triple overtime 45–37.

In 2004, however, Michigan put together one of its classic comebacks. Trailing 27–10 midway through the fourth quarter, the Wolverines scored 17 points in less than seven minutes to force overtime. Braylon Edwards caught two scoring passes from Chad Henne, and then in triple overtime he pulled in the winner in an incredible 45–37 victory on a wind-whipped afternoon.

Unbeaten State was salivating for its chance at East Lansing in 2005, and it was favored over Michigan for the first time in 37 years. Local police even had been posted to subdue the anticipated celebration. The Spartans erased a 21–7 deficit, and then forced overtime with a late touchdown on a 74-yard fumble return. But the Spartans' agony continued when a missed field goal in OT gave it to Michigan, 34–31.

A Nosedive in '05

Every team has a season in which the wheels come off. Even the great programs have the occasional losing year, such as Nebraska's 5–7 debacle in 2004. That left Michigan as the team with the most consecutive years without a losing season. Not since 1967 had the Wolverines tasted that vinegar. The closest they came was the 6–6 campaign in 1984.

But for a while in 2005, it appeared that streak could end. Tailback Mike Hart and offensive tackle Jake Long, among the best in the conference at their positions, went down with injuries. Except for easy wins over inferior opponents, every game was a struggle. By week six, the Wolverines were 3–3.

Notre Dame beat them 17–10 after Henne fumbled near the Irish goal line. Wisconsin came back on them in the last quarter in a 23–20 defeat. Minnesota, which appeared to be running out the clock for overtime, inexplicably broke loose on a long outside run, then kicked a field goal with seconds left to win 23–20.

The offense could not find a rhythm, and the defense couldn't stiffen in the close games. But somehow the Wolverines righted the ship, won four in a row, and went into the Ohio State game with an outside shot at a conference title. However, quarterback Troy Smith did it to Michigan for the second straight year, bringing

Minnesota wide receiver Jared Ellerson hoists the Little Brown Jug after defeating Michigan in 2005. U-M had held on to the trophy since 1986, winning 16 straight games.

Desperate to score on the last play of the Alamo Bowl, Mike Hart laterals the ball. Nebraska won 32–28, concluding Michigan's first five-loss season in 21 years.

the Buckeyes down the field for two late touchdowns in a 25–21 victory. This fourth loss of the year sent Michigan to the Alamo Bowl and a date with Nebraska.

The Huskers had rebounded from their own down year, finishing 7–4 and looking to a bowl win for vindication. It was just more of the same for the Wolverines in San Antonio, as they lost a late lead and trailed 32–28. In one of the most bizarre bowl endings ever, Michigan players lateralled the ball downfield after the clock ran out as the Nebraska subs came pouring off the bench in celebration. Both parties barely missed becoming entangled, avoiding a replay of the infamous California-Stanford band-on-the-field finale.

The disheartening losses persuaded Lloyd Carr to revamp his coaching staff. New coordinators were named on both offense and defense. Ron English, who had accepted a job with the Chicago Bears, was persuaded to resign and return to rescue the sagging Michigan defense.

Big Blue Resurgence

By the third week of the 2006 season, memories of the previous year's plummet had all but evaporated. Michigan went down to South Bend for its first road game in a place that had always given the Wolverines problems. Notre Dame was expected to contend for a national title with senior quarterback Brady Quinn running coach Charlie Weis's pro-style offense.

Yet Michigan handed the Irish one of the worst beatings of their series, a 47–21 stomping. Mario Manningham caught just four passes on the day, but three of them went for touchdowns. Quinn seemed baffled by a Michigan rush that came at him from all directions, with an aggressive blitz package that the Wolverines hadn't employed in years.

Michigan followed up with an impressive 27–13 win over Wisconsin, the only loss that the Badgers suffered all year. From there it was a quick ride through the rest of the schedule. Defending champion Penn State gave Michigan a tough 17–10 game at Happy Valley. But after the Notre Dame game, no one was able to score more than 14 points on this suddenly formidable defense.

Curiously enough, it was Ball State—scheduled as a fill-in for an early November date—that gave Michigan its toughest time. An ordinary Mid-American Conference team, the Cardinals unleashed a passing attack that had Michigan on its heels much of the afternoon. They actually threatened to tie the game late before losing 34–26.

But that was an aberration. With all their stars healthy and with the new-look defense, the Wolverines rose to No. 2 in the polls. The only team ahead of them? Ohio State. They were the only major unbeaten teams remaining in the country, and as the calendar moved through November it seemed that the national championship would come down to their meeting at Ohio Stadium. It was the first time since the fateful 10–10 tie of 1973 that both teams were undefeated and untied—and the first time the teams ever met while ranked first and second.

Then, just one day before kickoff, Bo Schembechler passed away.

Running back Brandon Minor dives into the end zone against Ball State. The Cardinals surprisingly gave Michigan a scare before falling short late in the game.

Game of the Century

After Michigan scored ten third-quarter points to make it 28–24 Ohio State, Antonio Pittman ripped off this 56-yard touchdown run to give the Buckeyes a comfortable cushion.

The super-hyped 2006 Michigan-Ohio State game confounded every prediction. In a series noted for its tense defensive struggles, the offenses ran wild. For the third straight season, Troy Smith baffled the Wolverines with his ability to frustrate the rush and his knack for hitting his receivers on the dead run. He threw three touchdown passes in the first half, staking the Buckeyes to a 28–14 lead at intermission.

Michigan scored the first ten points of the second half, and 19 seconds into the fourth quarter a Mike Hart touchdown cut the Buckeyes' lead to four points, 35–31. But OSU had an answer for every Wolverine rally, and Smith's touchdown pass to Brian Robiskie with 5:38 left made it an 11-point margin again. When Ohio State recovered an onside kick after a late Michigan touchdown and two-point conversion, the Buckeyes prevailed 42–39.

The game thrilled the Ohio State crowd, which had stood for a moment of silence in a moving tribute to the recently departed Bo Schembechler before kickoff. It also drew huge TV ratings, and the clamor grew for a rematch in the BCS National Championship Game. It gathered strength after Southern Cal was upset by UCLA. But once-beaten Florida won the Southeastern Conference title game to narrowly edge out Michigan in the BCS standings. The Gators then proved emphatically that they were the worthiest challenger by routing OSU 41–14 in the national title game.

Michigan settled for the Rose Bowl and another date with the Trojans. It was a measure of how the BCS had changed the game since 1997 that the former prime goal of Michigan football was now regarded as a consolation prize.

The Consolation Game

Two angry teams met in Pasadena in January 2007. Southern Cal players had been kicking themselves after dropping their season finale to UCLA, which deprived them of a title shot. Michigan felt it had been jobbed out of the rematch it deserved with Ohio State. In addition to all that, Michigan's top alumnus, former President Gerald Ford, died a few days before the game.

Michigan simply could not stop Southern Cal's aerial attack and went down meekly, 32–18. John David Booty picked apart the Michigan secondary while Chad Henne was sacked six times by a USC rush that also managed to hold Hart in check. The 74 points given up in the final two games raised new doubts about Michigan's defense. Nevertheless, for good and bad, it was a season to remember.

All-American Grunts

It always begins with the offensive line at Michigan. Year after year, the glamour backs can count on the big guys up front to clear the way.

The combination of Matt Elliott and Greg "The Barge" Skrepenak was a versatile and durable force during the 1990 and '91 seasons. Elliott played both guard and center during his career, and Skrepenak, a 322-pounder, started 48 consecutive games—then a Michigan record for an offensive lineman. He made All-American teams as a junior and senior.

Steve Everitt continued the tradition of outstanding Michigan centers. He was voted the top Wolverine at that position from 1969 to 2000, and he was chosen with the 14th pick of the 1993 NFL draft. That was the highest of any Michigan offensive lineman during this period.

Jon Jansen was one of the bulwarks of the 1997 title team, which depended on ball-control offense to win. He broke Skrepenak's record by making 50 consecutive starts at right tackle, and he was named the top offensive lineman in the Big Ten in 1998.

Steve Hutchinson was a two-time All-American guard (1999–2000). He went through his final two seasons without ever allowing a sack, and he

Defensive tackle Chris Hutchinson (pictured) is one of five Michigan players with 24 or 25 career sacks. Highest on the sack list is Mark Messner—with 36.

was named All-Big Ten all four years. All-American Chris Hutchinson was Big Ten Defensive Lineman of the Year in 1992, the year he tied a school record with 11 sacks.

Jake Long, a mammoth presence at 6'7", 315 pounds, has been called the best of all offensive tackles to play for Michigan. A crushing blocker whose size belies his speed, Long was considered the best at his position in America in 2006 and 2007.

The defense had its share of stars, too. Jarrett Irons, with an unerring instinct for the ball, was a standout linebacker on the 1995–96 teams. He ranks second in career tackles with 440. Right behind him in this stat is linebacker Erick Anderson. He was recruited as a fullback but soon found a home on the other side of the ball. He led the team in tackles four straight years (1988–91) and was Michigan's first Butkus Award winner.

Complementing Charles Woodson on the outstanding 1997 defense was end Glen Steele, a sack artist who was voted best defensive lineman on that team. James Hall also starred at defensive end. He trailed only Mark Messner in career sacks with 25 when he concluded his career in 1999.

Jake Long, an enormous, bruising offensive tackle, blew open holes for running back Mike Hart for four years. In 2006 and '07, he was a consensus first-team All-American.

Roller-Coaster Ride

Describing the 2007 season as tumultuous doesn't even begin to capture the upheaval that swept across Michigan football. It started with one of the biggest upsets in college football history and two straight humiliations in the Big House. It ended with a stirring bowl victory and the start of an entirely new coaching era. In between, there was an eight-game winning streak and crippling injuries to offensive stars Chad Henne and Mike Hart.

Appalachian State was chosen as the opening day opponent in Ann Arbor because of Michigan's failure to land a team from a major conference. The defending Division I-AA champs weren't supposed to give Michigan much of a tussle. Instead, the Wolverines were befuddled by the Moun-

Players carry Lloyd Carr off the field following Michigan's surprising win in the Capital One Bowl—Carr's last game as head coach.

taineers' spread offense and lost on a game-ending blocked field goal, 34–32. The defeat sent shock waves through the program and all of football.

The following week, Oregon brought its version of the spread to the Big House and wiped out the Wolverines 39–7, Michigan's worst defeat in years. Coach Lloyd Carr was booed loudly by the big crowd, and so was Henne. No one knew it yet, but Carr already had informed Athletic Director Bill Martin that this was to be his last season.

Despite the 0–2 start, Carr still managed to right the ship. Michigan routed a bad Notre Dame team and swept through the conference schedule, beating Penn State and

Rose Bowl-bound Illinois and pulling off a comeback victory over Michigan State. Eventually, injuries caught up with the Wolverines. They lost at Wisconsin and once again, maddeningly, to Ohio State, 14–3. Henne was unable to throw, Hart's cutting ability was hampered in the slick conditions, and Michigan could never mount an offensive threat in the game.

In the Capital One Bowl, Michigan was a ten-point underdog to the defending national champion, Florida. But with everyone finally healthy, the Wolverines showed what might have been in this bizarre season. They upset the Gators 41–35 to send Carr out a jubilant winner.

A New Era Begins

The search for Lloyd Carr's successor became an embarrassment when Bill Martin could not make a deal with either Les Miles (Louisiana State's head coach) or Greg Schiano (head coach at Rutgers). But just as it was shaping up as a genuine fiasco, Martin came up with Rich Rodriguez, an offensive wizard who had turned West Virginia into a national power as its

Head coach Rich Rodriguez

head coach. Rodriguez promised to bring his version of the spread, which Michigan had so much trouble trying to stop, to Ann Arbor for 2008.

It was just the third time in 70 years that Michigan had gone outside the program, and it also marked the end of the 39-season Bo Schembechler era. The departure of the highly popular Rodriguez, a native of West Virginia and a former player there, sparked some ugly protests across that state. But it was the beginning of an entirely new football philosophy at Michigan.

The Record Book

The Victors and Best

- Overall record: 869–286–36 (.745)
- Big Ten record: 461–162–18 (.733)
- Total points scored: Michigan 29,401, Opponents 12,776
- National championships (11): 1901, 1902, 1903, 1904, 1918, 1923, 1932, 1933, 1947, 1948, 1997
- Conference championships (42): 1898, 1901–04, 1906, 1918, 1922–23, 1925–26, 1930–33, 1943, 1947–50, 1964, 1969, 1971–74, 1976–78, 1980, 1982, 1986, 1988–92, 1997–98, 2000, 2003–04

Tops in the Nation

Michigan holds NCAA Division I–A records for:

- Most victories (869)
- Highest all-time winning percentage (.745)
- Most winning seasons (110)
- Most undefeated seasons (23)
- Greatest overall margin of victory (16,625 points)
- Most conference championships (42)
- Longest streak of bowl game appearances (33; active)
- Largest stadium (107,501)
- Longest streak of home attendance in excess of 100,000 (208 games, active)
- Largest attendance at a single game (112,118 on 11/22/03 vs. Ohio St.)

Other notable achievements:

- Longest active streak of nonlosing seasons (40)
- Longest active streak of scoring in a game (288 games, dating back to 10/20/84)
- Best uniform in sports, according to an ESPN.com poll that generated more than seven million votes

Annual Records

Year	Coach	Overall W–L–T	Conf. W–L–T	Bowl	U-M Pts.	Opp. Pts.
1879	—	1–0–1	—	—	1	0
1880	—	1–0–0	—	—	13	6
1881	—	0–3–0	—	—	4	28
1882	—	No Games				
1883	—	2–3–0	—	—	63	73
1884	—	2–0–0	—	—	36	10
1885	—	3–0–0	—	—	82	0
1886	—	2–0–0	—	—	74	0
1887	—	3–0–0	—	—	66	0
1888	—	4–1–0	—	—	130	46
1889	—	1–2–0	—	—	33	80
1890	—	4–1–0	—	—	129	36
1891	Murphy & Crawford	4–5–0	—	—	168	114
1892	Barbour	7–5–0	—	—	298	170
1893	Barbour	7–3–0	—	—	278	102
1894	McCauley	9–1–1	—	—	244	84
1895	McCauley	8–1–0	—	—	266	14
1896	Ward	9–1–0	2–1–0 T2	—	262	11
1897	Ferbert	6–1–1	2–1–0 3	—	166	31
1898	Ferbert	10–0–0	3–0–0 T1	—	205	26
1899	Ferbert	8–2–0	1–1–0 T3	—	176	43
1900	Lea	7–2–1	3–2–0 5	—	117	55
1901	Yost	11–0–0	4–0–0 T1	Rose	550	0
1902	Yost	11–0–0	5–0–0 1	—	644	12

Year	Coach	Overall W–L–T	Conf. W–L–T	Bowl	U-M Pts.	Opp. Pts.	Year	Coach	Overall W–L–T	Conf. W–L–T	Bowl	U-M Pts.	Opp. Pts.
1903	Yost	11–0–1	3–0–1 T1	—	565	6	1939	Crisler	6–2–0	3–2–0 T4	—	219	94
1904	Yost	10–0–0	2–0–0 T1	—	567	22	1940	Crisler	7–1–0	3–1–0 2	—	196	34
1905	Yost	12–1–0	2–1–0 T2	—	495	2	1941	Crisler	6–1–1	3–1–1 T2	—	147	41
1906	Yost	4–1–0	1–0–0 T1	—	72	30	1942	Crisler	7–3–0	3–2–0 T3	—	221	134
1907	Yost	5–1–0	—	—	107	6	1943	Crisler	8 1 0	6 0 0 T1	—	302	73
1908	Yost	5–2–1	—	—	128	81	1944	Crisler	8–2–0	5–2–0 2	—	204	91
1909	Yost	6–1–0	—	—	115	34	1945	Crisler	7–3–0	5–1–0 2	—	187	99
1910	Yost	3–0–3	—	—	29	9	1946	Crisler	6 2 1	5 1 1 2	—	233	73
1911	Yost	5–1–2	—	—	90	38	1947	Crisler	10–0–0	6–0–0 1	Rose	394	53
1912	Yost	5–2–0	—	—	158	65	1948	Oosterbaan	9–0–0	6–0–0 1	—	252	44
1913	Yost	6–1–T	—	—	175	21	1949	Oosterbaan	6–2–1	4–1–1 T1	—	135	85
1914	Yost	6–3–0	—	—	233	68	1950	Oosterbaan	6–3–1	4–1–1 1	Rose	150	114
1915	Yost	4–3–1	—	—	130	81	1951	Oosterbaan	4–5–0	4–2–0 4	—	135	122
1916	Yost	7–2–0	—	—	253	56	1952	Oosterbaan	5–4–0	4–2–0 T4	—	207	134
1917	Yost	8–2–0	0–1–0 T8	—	304	53	1953	Oosterbaan	6–3–0	3–3–0 T5	—	163	101
1918	Yost	5–0–0	2–0–0 T1	—	96	6	1954	Oosterbaan	6–3–0	5–2–0 T2	—	139	87
1919	Yost	3–4–0	1–4–0 T7	—	93	102	1955	Oosterbaan	7–2–0	5–2–0 3	—	179	94
1920	Yost	5–2–0	2–2–0 6	—	121	21	1956	Oosterbaan	7–2–0	5–2–0 2	—	233	123
1921	Yost	5–1–1	2–1–1 5	—	187	21	1957	Oosterbaan	5–3–1	3–3–1 6	—	187	147
1922	Yost	6–0–1	4–0–0 T1	—	183	13	1958	Oosterbaan	2–6–1	1–5–1 8	—	132	211
1923	Yost	8–0–0	4–0–0 T1	—	150	12	1959	Elliott	4–5–0	3–4–0 7	—	122	161
1924	Little	6–2–0	4–2–0 4	—	155	54	1960	Elliott	5–4–0	2–4–0 T5	—	133	84
1925	Yost	7–1–0	5–1–0 1	—	227	3	1961	Elliott	6–3–0	3–3–0 6	—	212	163
1926	Yost	7–1–0	5–0–0 T1	—	191	38	1962	Elliott	2–7–0	1–6–0 10	—	70	214
1927	Wieman	6–2–0	3–2–0 3	—	137	39	1963	Elliott	3–4–2	2–3–2 T5	—	131	127
1928	Wieman	3–4–1	2–3–0 T7	—	36	62	1964	Elliott	9–1–0	6 1 0 1	Rose	235	83
1929	Kipke	5–3–1	1–3–1 T7	—	109	75	1965	Elliott	4–6–0	2–5–0 T7	—	185	161
1930	Kipke	8–0–1	5–0–0 T1	—	111	23	1966	Elliott	6–4–0	4–3–0 T3	—	236	138
1931	Kipke	8 1 1	5 1 0 T1	—	181	27	1967	Elliott	4–6–0	3–4–0 T5	—	144	179
1932	Kipke	8–0–0	6–0–0 T1	—	123	13	1968	Elliott	8–2–0	6–1–0 2	—	277	155
1933	Kipke	7–0–1	5–0–1 T1	—	131	18	1969	Schembechler	8–3–0	6–1–0 T1	Rose	352	148
1934	Kipke	1–7–0	0–6–0 10	—	21	143	1970	Schembechler	9–1–0	6–1–0 T2	—	288	90
1935	Kipke	4–4–0	2–3–0 T5	—	68	131	1971	Schembechler	11–1–0	8–0–0 1	Rose	421	83
1936	Kipke	1–7–0	0–5–0 T8	—	36	127	1972	Schembechler	10–1–0	7–1–0 T1	—	264	57
1937	Kipke	4–4–0	3–3–0 T4	—	54	110	1973	Schembechler	10–0–1	7–0–1 T1	—	330	68
1938	Crisler	6–1–1	3–1–1 T2	—	131	40	1974	Schembechler	10–1–0	7–1–0 T1	—	324	75

Year	Coach	Overall W–L–T	Conf. W–L–T	Bowl	U-M Pts.	Opp. Pts.
1975	Schembechler	8–2–2	7–1–0 2	Orange	324	130
1976	Schembechler	10–2–0	7–1–0 T1	Rose	432	95
1977	Schembechler	10–2–0	7–1–0 T1	Rose	353	124
1978	Schembechler	10–2–0	7–1–0 T1	Rose	372	105
1979	Schembechler	8–4–0	6–2–0 3	Gator	312	151
1980	Schembechler	10–2–0	8–0–0 1	Rose	322	129
1981	Schembechler	9–3–0	6–3–0 T3	Blue-bonnet	355	162
1982	Schembechler	8–4–0	8–1–0 1	Rose	345	204
1983	Schembechler	9–3–0	8–1–0 2	Sugar	355	160
1984	Schembechler	6–6–0	5–4–0 T6	Holiday	214	200
1985	Schembechler	10–1–1	6–1–1 2	Fiesta	342	98
1986	Schembechler	11–2–0	7–1–0 T1	Rose	379	203
1987	Schembechler	8–4–0	5–3–0 4	Hall of Fame	331	172
1988	Schembechler	9–2–1	7–0–1 1	Rose	361	167
1989	Schembechler	10–2–0	8–0–0 1	Rose	335	184
1990	Moeller	9–3–0	6–2–0 T1	Gator	389	198
1991	Moeller	10–2–0	8–0–0 1	Rose	420	203
1992	Moeller	9–0–3	6–0–2 1	Rose	431	171
1993	Moeller	8–4–0	5–3–0 T4	Hall of Fame	342	160
1994	Moeller	8–4–0	5–3–0 3	Holiday	330	268
1995	Carr	9–4–0	5–3–0 T3	Alamo	338	223
1996	Carr	8–4–0	5–3–0 T5	Outback	277	184
1997	Carr	12–0–0	8–0–0 1	Rose	322	114
1998	Carr	10–3–0	7–1–0 T1	Citrus	359	235
1999	Carr	10–2–0	6–2–0 T2	Orange	361	247
2000	Carr	9–3–0	6–2–0 T1	Citrus	404	229
2001	Carr	8–4–0	6–2–0 2	Citrus	320	237
2002	Carr	10–3–0	6–2–0 3	Outback	361	265
2003	Carr	10–3–0	7–1–0 1	Rose	460	219
2004	Carr	9–3–0	7–1–0 T1	Rose	370	279
2005	Carr	7–5–0	5–3–0 T3	Alamo	345	244
2006	Carr	11–2–0	7–1–0 T2	Rose	380	207
2007	Carr	9–4–0	6–2–0 T2	Capital One	354	278

Head Coaches

Coach	Years	W–L–T	Pct.
Mike Murphy and Frank Crawford	1891	4–5–0	.444
Frank Barbour	1892–93	14–8–0	.636
William McCauley	1894–95	17–2–1	.875
William Ward	1896	9–1–0	.900
Gustave Ferbert	1897–99	24–3–1	.875
Langdon Lea	1900	7–2–1	.750
Fielding Yost	1901–23, 1925–26	165–29–10	.833
George Little	1924	6–2–0	.750
Elton Wieman	1927–28	9–6–1	.594
Harry Kipke	1929–37	46–26–4	.632
Fritz Crisler	1938–47	71–16–3	.806
Bennie Oosterbaan	1948–58	63–33–4	.650
Bump Elliott	1959–68	51–42–2	.547
Bo Schembechler	1969–89	194–48–5	.796
Gary Moeller	1990–94	44–13–3	.758
Lloyd Carr	1995–2007	122–40–0	.753

Bowl Game Results

Season	Bowl	Result
1901	Rose	U-M 49, Stanford 0
1947	Rose	U-M 49, USC 0
1950	Rose	U-M 14, California 6
1964	Rose	U-M 34, Oregon St. 7
1969	Rose	USC 10, U-M 3
1971	Rose	Stanford 13, U-M 12
1975	Orange	Oklahoma 14, U-M 6
1976	Rose	USC 14, U-M 6
1977	Rose	Washington 27, U-M 20
1978	Rose	USC 17, U-M 10
1979	Gator	North Carolina 17, U-M 15
1980	Rose	U-M 23, Washington 6
1981	Bluebonnet	U-M 33, UCLA 14
1982	Rose	UCLA 24, U-M 14
1983	Sugar	Auburn 9, U-M 7
1984	Holiday	Brigham Young 24, U-M 17

Season	Bowl	Result
1985	Fiesta	U-M 27, Nebraska 23
1986	Rose	Arizona St. 22, U-M 15
1987	Hall of Fame	U-M 28, Alabama 24
1988	Rose	U-M 22, USC 14
1989	Rose	USC 17, U-M 10
1990	Gator	U-M 35, Mississippi 3
1991	Rose	Washington 34, U-M 14
1992	Rose	U-M 38, Washington 31
1993	Hall of Fame	U-M 42, North Carolina St. 7
1994	Holiday	U-M 24, Colorado St. 14
1995	Alamo	Texas A&M 22, U-M 20
1996	Outback	Alabama 17, U-M 14
1997	Rose	U-M 21, Washington St. 16
1998	Citrus	U-M 45, Arkansas 31
1999	Orange	U-M 35, Alabama 34 (OT)
2000	Citrus	U-M 31, Auburn 28
2001	Citrus	Tennessee 45, U-M 17
2002	Outback	U-M 38, Florida 30
2003	Rose	USC 28, U-M 14
2004	Rose	Texas 38, U-M 37
2005	Alamo	Nebraska 32, U-M 28
2006	Rose	USC 32, U-M 18
2007	Capital One	U-M 41, Florida 35

Heisman Trophy Winners

Tom Harmon, 1940   Charles Woodson, 1997
Desmond Howard, 1991

Heisman Runner-ups

Tom Harmon, 2nd in 1939   Anthony Carter, 4th in 1982
Bob Chappuis, 2nd in 1947   Jim Harbaugh, 3rd in 1986
Bob Timberlake, 4th in 1964   Chris Perry, 4th in 2003
Rob Lytle, 3rd in 1976   Mike Hart, 5th in 2006
Rick Leach, 3rd in 1978

Retired Numbers

#11 Albert Wistert, Alvin Wistert, Francis Wistert
#47 Bennie Oosterbaan   #87 Ron Kramer
#48 Gerald Ford   #98 Tom Harmon

Members of College Football Hall of Fame

Albert Benbrook, Willie Heston, Merv Pregulman
Dave Brown, Elroy Hirsch, Bo Schembechler
Anthony Carter, Ron Johnson, Germany Schulz
Bob Chappuis, Harry Kipke, Neil Snow
Fritz Crisler, Ron Kramer, Ernie Vick
Tom Curtis, George Little, Bob Westfall
Dan Dierdorf, Jim Mandich, Tad Wieman
Bump Elliott, Johnny Maulbetsch, Albert Wistert
Pete Elliott, Reggie McKenize, Alvin Wistert
Benny Friedman, Harry Newman, Francis Wistert
Tom Harmon, Bennie Oosterbaan, Fielding Yost

Career Rushing Yards

1) Mike Hart 5,040   6) Chris Perry 3,696
2) Anthony Thomas 4,472   7) Rob Lytle 3,317
3) Jamie Morris 4,393   8) Billy Taylor 3,072
4) Tyrone Wheatley 4,178   9) Gordon Bell 2,900
5) Butch Woolfolk 3,861   10) Tim Biakabutuka 2,810

Career Passing Yards

1) Chad Henne 9,715   6) Tom Brady 5,351
2) John Navarre 9,254   7) Steve Smith 4,860
3) Elvis Grbac 6,460   8) Brian Griese 4,383
4) Todd Collins 5,858   9) Rick Leach 4,284
5) Jim Harbaugh 5,449   10) John Wangler 2,994

Career Receiving Yards

1) Braylon Edwards 3,541   6) Tai Streets 2,284
2) Anthony Carter 3,076   7) Marquise Walker 2,269
3) Amani Toomer 2,657   8) Jason Avant 2,247
4) David Terrell 2,317   9) Greg McMurtry 2,163
5) Mario Manningham 2,310   10) Desmond Howard 2,146

Career Scoring

1) Garrett Rivas, PK   354
2) Anthony Thomas, RB 336
3) Tyrone Wheatley, RB 324
4) Mike Gillette, PK   307
5) Remy Hamilton, PK   280
6) Mike Hart, RB   258

Career Tackles*

1) Ron Simpkins   516
2) Jarrett Irons   440
3) Erick Anderson   428
4) Paul Girgash   414
5) Mike Mallory   396
6) Andy Cannavino   385

* since 1966

Career Sacks*

1) Mark Messier   36
2) James Hall   25
3) Chris Hutchinson   24
3) Jason Horn   24
3) Glen Steele   24
3) LaMarr Woodley   24

* since 1980

Career Interceptions

1) Tom Curtis   25
2) Charles Woodson   18
3) Wally Teninga   13
4) Gene Derricotte   12
4) Brad Cochran   12
4) Leon Hall   12

Michigan Rushing Records

- Most rushing yards, season: 1,818, Tim Biakabutuka (1995)
- Most rushing yards, game: 347, Ron Johnson (11/16/68 vs. Wisconsin)
- Most rushing touchdowns, career: 55, Anthony Thomas
- Most rushing touchdowns, season: 19, Ron Johnson (1968)
- Most rushing touchdowns, game: 5, Ron Johnson (11/16/68 vs. Wisconsin)
- Highest rushing average, career: Jon Vaughn, 6.29
- Highest rushing average, season: Tyrone Wheatley, 7.34 (1992)
- Longest run from scrimmage: 92 yards, Butch Woolfolk (11/3/79 vs. Wisconsin)
- Most games with at least 100 rushing yards, career: 27, Mike Hart
- Most games with at least 200 rushing yards, career: 5, Mike Hart

Michigan Passing Records

- Most passing completions, career: 828, Chad Henne
- Most passing completions, season: 270, John Navarre (2003)
- Most passing completions, game: 34, Tom Brady (1/1/00 vs. Alabama in Orange Bowl)
- Most passing yards, season: 3,331, John Navarre (2003)
- Most passing yards, game: 389, John Navarre (10/4/03 vs. Iowa)
- Most passing touchdowns, career: 87, Chad Henne
- Most passing touchdowns, season: 25, Elvis Grbac (1991) and Chad Henne (2004)
- Most passing touchdowns, game: 4, achieved 17 times
- Longest pass completion: 97 yards, Ryan Mallett to Mario Manningham (11/10/07 vs. Wisconsin)

Michigan Receiving Records

- Most receptions, career: 252, Braylon Edwards
- Most receptions, season: 97, Braylon Edwards (2004)
- Most receptions, game: 15, Marquise Walker (9/8/01 vs. Washington and 11/24/01 vs. Ohio State)
- Most receiving yards, season: 1,330, Braylon Edwards (2004)
- Most receiving yards, game: 197, Jack Clancy (9/17/66 vs. Oregon State)
- Most touchdown receptions, career: 39, Braylon Edwards
- Most touchdown receptions, season: 19, Desmond Howard (1991)
- Most touchdown receptions, game: 4, Derrick Alexander (10/24/92 vs. Minnesota)
- Longest pass reception: 97 yards, Mario Manningham from Ryan Mallett (10/10/07 vs. Wisconsin)

Michigan Miscellaneous Records

- Most kickoff return yards, career: 1,993, Steve Breaston
- Most kickoff return touchdowns, career: 2, Desmond Howard
- Most punt return yards, career: 1,599, Steve Breaston
- Most punt return touchdowns, career: 4, Gene Derricotte, Derrick Alexander, and Steve Breaston
- Most field goals, career: 64, Garrett Rivas
- Highest punting average, career: 42.8, Monte Robbins

Index